Dogma's Primrose Path

John L. Martinez

Hamilton Books

An Imprint of
Rowman & Littlefield

Lanham • Boulder • New York • Toronto • Plymouth, UK

Copyright © 2015 by Hamilton Books
4501 Forbes Boulevard, Suite 200, Lanham, Maryland 20706
Hamilton Books Aquisitions Department (301) 459-3366

Unit A, Whitacre Mews, 26-34 Stannary Street,
London SE11 4AB, United Kingdom

All rights reserved

British Library Cataloguing in Publication Information Available

Library of Congress Control Number: 2014958244
ISBN: 978-0-7618-6532-2 (pbk : alk. paper)—ISBN: 978-0-7618-6633-9 (electronic)

To Mom and Dad
Who are no more
But whose approval
I shall always seek

Contents

Introduction		vii
1	The Self	1
2	Religion and God: The Disconnect between Religion and God	11
3	Wealth	47
4	Nation-State Lawlessness	85
Conclusion		103

Introduction

The great majority of opinion is that things will never really change—that war, enslavement, exploitation, ignorance and poverty are permanent fixtures in humankind's experience. Custom and tradition continually reinforce the notion that because we are stuck with our deficient human natures, we must resign ourselves to a history and a world of constant misery, greed, and violence. Human nature becomes the culprit or scapegoat. It is a premise of this volume that the inevitableness of this perceived state of affairs is only a learned notion and is otherwise baseless. There is no sound reason or genuine rule of nature to support this dismal and self-prophetic belief. This volume maintains that religious and secular dogmas are the villains in this never-ending tragedy. And, interestingly, in all this darkness of human history there are always scattered bright pockets of wealth and privilege that, pursuant to some overpowering social physics, we have been told are inevitable.

The task of the human organism, like all organisms, is to successfully navigate itself through life. For our purposes the journey of the human species may be viewed as beginning long ago at the stage of instinct and thereafter venturing forward to begin a process of incorporating reason, along with instinct, as a necessary life tool. Unfortunately the journey toward reason has been disrupted, and we now live in a world almost completely enveloped by dogma. We are effectively in the darkness of Plato's cave where we think we perceive substance but only see shadows. What passes so often for real thinking is the regurgitation of dogma, grand authoritative ideas that provide us with soothing and simplistic conclusions but have no real basis in fact or reason.

It is a premise of this book that a world free of dogma would be a better world, a rational world, a world of hope and fairness. If our species is ever to fulfill its collective promise it must, to borrow a Kantian expression, awaken from its "dogmatic slumber." To simply and continually rely on inherited, unwarranted and biased custom and tradition is incompatible with our species' natural progression. The need to free ourselves from dogma and dogmatic applications is not a matter of choice or preference but of necessity. If profound change does not occur nature dictates the continued stunting of the individual human being and perhaps the premature self-inflicted demise of our species.

Many believe that the miseries of the world emerge from our own defective human nature. But the obstacles to a truly better world do not emanate from our human nature. Civilization can be changed in a manner that will better give to each human an opportunity to fulfill his or her self-determined destiny. In this matter we are talking about profound change, the only change that can actually get the job done. In order to accomplish this, we as humans have got to get beyond ourselves and overcome deeply ingrained dogmatic ideas, values, and traditions. Accepting and meeting this challenge is a necessary precondition to our species being able to thrive and grow naturally in this world we find ourselves a part of. We must be brave but mature, adventuresome but realistic, and above all we must be confident that posterity will forever be in our debt.

There are three profound conditions facing our species: (1) religious belief, (2) inordinate wealth among the few, and (3) the inherent lawlessness of the nation-state system. If they are not overcome humankind is surely doomed to the horrors of the present and the past. Changing these conditions is difficult, both because we have a normal resistance to change and because those who are against change are the smartest, most wealthy and powerful, and the most esteemed and well thought of among us. The foes of change all share something in common: They all share a vested interest in the continuance of today's mess.

How do these three conditions prevent the embrace of reason and contribute to the misery of the world? First, religious belief constitutes a grotesque situation where adults cling to a fairy tale learned as children. Make believe forms the basis of their lifelong orientation that contorts their thinking and causes them to live in a distorted non-real world. On a global level the effect of competing and contradictory religious dogmas has caused, encouraged, or facilitated much of the horrors and violence documented throughout the course of human history. Second, inordinate wealth in the few is in and of itself obscene. That some members of our species live in great wealth and most live in great poverty can never be reconciled. But beyond the ethical, inordinate wealth in the few invariably leads to the manipulation of government, in every society, and throughout all time. When the primary agenda of any government is to service the wealthy the public interest is dismissed, usually in the name of conveniently selected economic or political dogma. From the divine right of kings we have progressed to the divine right of the inordinately wealthy few. Third, the nation-state guarantees the absence of the rule of law globally and ensures the continued presence of wars and violence, dominance and exploitation. The present condition of so-called "sovereign" nations is based on power, will, and design. Within this nonsystematic grouping, the rule of law, which is our only hope for peace and progress, can never have a true and meaningful place.

Each of these three conditions is enabled because of the use of dogma. *Dogma* (sometimes called ideology) is a false belief system that convinces those who are harmed by a policy to nonetheless support that policy. It is promulgated through scare tactics, promoted by a relentless indoctrination of the youth of the world, and nurtured by a wealth of traditions and lore that makes the false belief seem natural and unquestionable. Dogma cannot be supported by reason, common sense, or experience. Since dogma's claims do not rely on reason or logic, it is impenetrable from direct challenge by fact, experience, reason, or logic. It is simply immune from all rational and mature discourse. It is, however, vulnerable to individual, personal growth and development. In the chapters that follow, we will examine how these three conditions endure and thrive while resting on pillars of dogmatic belief.

Chapter One

The Self

"The universe, that is, the whole mass of all things that are, is corporeal, that is to say, body . . . consequently every part of the universe, is body, and that which is not body, is no part of the universe." —Thomas Hobbs, 1651

Humans are the authors of our own miseries. In the perpetuation of poverty and war, we play a dualistic role, a role that is marked by a mutual and oscillatory relationship between ourselves as individuals on the one hand and ourselves collectively as institutions, traditions, and ideologies on the other. This dual role means that we are both actors and acted upon: On one hand as individuals we endorse and perpetuate institutions, and on the other we are molded and shaped by them. This human plasticity was noted by Rousseau many years ago. He held that members of civil society were as they were not because of their naturally deficient or evil natures but because of how they were raised and taught by society itself. Hence, he rejected the notion of a naturally defective human nature and understood societies' contributory role in the creation of these underdeveloped and unfulfilled human beings in civil society.

Our goal for these institutions should be to create a societal environment conducive to and directed toward the natural healthy human development of all members of society and not just the privileged few. But we have been led to believe that a supposedly defective human nature makes this impossible. Through dogmatic belief systems, societal institutions have long reinforced the notion that human nature and behavior cannot be sufficiently altered but only contained—and this through strict temporal custom and sanctions that pertain to both life and the afterlife. However, it is clear that we cannot be healthy and rational while functioning in a society whose institutions and conventions are not healthy and rational. We cannot be what we potentially can be if these institutions and conventions do not properly take into account who and what we are as human beings. If we see ourselves in primarily mythical, exaggerated, or distorted ways—for example, if selected groups within society see themselves in primarily negative, inferior, and unworthy ways—we can never have the healthy development of all people that should be our goal.

It is our social institutions and traditions that are primary contributors to these distortions. These ill-fitted institutions and traditions will inexorably produce the artificial and stunted individual and the societal cancers of unnecessary and exaggerated bias, fear, distrust, and selfishness. These same cancerous consequences, ironically but sadly, in turn, help perpetuate individual, devout, and loyal support for these same failed institutions and traditions. Because of the dualistic roles that we play, real change is extremely problematic. Change is like a fast-moving merry-go-round that has too much force for most persons to jump on. For change to occur it must begin with the individual who has the intellectual honesty and the moral courage to go beyond himself. The individual is only a small constituent part of the whole and as such the whole is vulnerable only when a sufficient number of individual parts are sufficiently weary.

With regard to the dignity, spirit, and sanctity of the individual, old dogmatic traditions are nihilistic and constitute a gargantuan obstacle to a better future for all people. Although no one person alone can change the institutions that have so much influence in our lives, change must always start with the individual. It entails a thought process that successfully attacks itself, testing the assumptions the individual has received from the institutions and traditions around him or her. It requires the remaking of one's self. Only then is institutional change, however meager, possible. In the sections that follow, we examine approaches to remaking the self so that we can begin to challenge the institutions and traditions that are perpetuating the miseries of our world.

THE PHYSICAL SELF

The realness of life for earthly living creatures lies solely in its physicality. If anything is a something in our universe, it is a physical something or a something that exhibits physical properties or forces. Although this view seems to be compelled by science and logic it is not a new or novel idea. About four hundred years ago Hobbs in his *Leviathan* wrote that "the universe, that is, the whole mass of all things that are, is corporeal, that is to say, body; and hath the dimensions of magnitude, namely, length, breadth, and depth: also every part of body, is likewise body, and hath the like dimensions; and consequently every part of the universe, is body, and that which is not body, is no part of the universe."

For a physical being in our universe the nonphysical or the metaphysical can have no meaning or reality. We can experience the physical world because we are of the physical world. It follows that all that goes into the making of a human being is ultimately physical. Even energy production in the form of thoughts, emotions, and self-awareness is still a physical occurrence. All that we have previously been use to labeling "mental," "spirit," or "will," as opposed to that which we have traditionally labeled physical, is still ultimately physical. If our existence is predicated solely on our physical nature, it follows that for us as limited physical organisms it would not be possible to be cognizant of nonphysical realities or events. For the human organism there is nothing else but the physical universe. We are not equipped to experience any other world. Human beings can no more escape the limits of the physical universe than they can escape themselves.

Our physical universe, the only universe that for us is reality based, may be thought of as being divided into two physical forms, an inanimate one and an animate one. Animation is not detached or separate from the physical form. It is an expression or even a partial definition of that very form. Animation is an "expression" of the physical body because it is the natural and direct output of its own body. It in part defines body because any definition or description of this body without inclusion of its animated nature would be only partial and misleading. This animation that we may call "life" is therefore at the same time an expression of and a description of the physical corpus. It is inextricably bound up with its own corpus. Thought, emotions, and consciousness itself are types of animated physical events, forms or expressions. As one engages in thinking, what appears to oneself as images or pictures might appear to an outside viewer, peering into our cerebral and neurological systems from an external vantage point, simply as typical physical activity and energy production. Every thought or emotion is at the same time both produced from and is an aspect of the human body itself. Yes, the mental becomes the physical and the physical the mental. In fact they are one in the same. They are the same physical reality. What constitutes our every idea or component of our mental-psychological aspect is sent to and received by our one body. The rapidity and complexity of these oscillatory events is, of course, mind-boggling. Life, as a physical form or expression, is as much a part of the physical universe as any inanimate form or expression. This animated self is the living self.

The human "mental" processes of perception, thought, memory, and self awareness are tools of engagement by a physical creature existing in a physical world. These tools permit us to maneuver, survive, and perhaps flourish within our own physical world but not in any other world. Maneuvering through the natural world, utilizing all of our physical capabilities, is what we call life. It is experienced. In everyday language we might say that I or we experience. It may, however, be less inaccurate to say that experience is being experienced and that which is doing the experiencing, is actually experiencing itself. This dictates that there is not some object or thing, separate from experiencing, that already exists before the experiencing takes place that gets to do the experiencing. The body creates that which experiences and the body benefits from the experience to the extent that navigating through life is possible. Our bodies are essential to any experiencing that might be going on, both as impulse sender and receiver but it is what the body generates or creates that experiences. The reverberations from experiencing is surely felt by the active body, but the body as durable object is not engaging in the experiencing. We do not know why. We cannot explain it. But we do it. When we navigate through life, unencumbered by dogma and dogmatic patterns, we do it to the fullest extent of our capabilities. And in the end we at times are rewarded and enriched. We are as alive as we can be but no more than that.

Living and being, however precarious, and however much an engagement with the external world, in a Heideggerian sense, is both what we are and what we do. It is an aliveness that does not occur apart from body nor apart from the external world. Like a cozy fire, human life is a momentary and uncertain energy whose existence is always precarious and doubtful but whose existence is a true moment owned by the existent. Life is not diminished by this realistic view. Life will continue to be the same as humans cannot change our underlying reality. The demands of each day will continue as always. The rules of engagement will remain constant. We will each use the same physical attributes or abilities to continue to navigate through the same physical reality. And based on our familiarity with the unchanging past there will be no new and wondrous nonphysical miracle to relieve us from this physical reality.

What can be changed is our view and orientation about ourselves and our world. We can attempt to have a more realistic and objective view of what life is and can be, a view of life that is not distorted out of recognition by all too familiar dogma. Life, that which we experience, is still a gift, and it is still real. Life is not above or apart from the physical world. Life is a form or aspect of the physical world. Life for human beings would have no meaning or context without the physical world. We can only know what we call life through and by our bodies. I think of life as that soft warm illuminating energy pulsating immediately in and from body, earth, and stars. If everything is physical and if thought and consciousness are directly and immediately derived from body itself, this leaves no room or need for any separate and independent depository, container, or compartment for ideas, thoughts, and even self. These invented chambers have through time been typically called soul, self, or will. But we know that there is no homunculus or other detachable existent deep within the body.

Thoughts, ideas, mental pictures, emotions, memory, awareness of self and others, and the whole panoply of "mental" processes are but momentary events that are dependent and contingent upon bodily activity. They are not singularly durable phenomena in the same way our bodies and other objects are. They are consequences that owe their complete existence to bodies in motion. When our bodies are permanently stilled at death there is no longer any experiencing agent or event going on. Experiencing is not dead as is body; it is simply no longer. The unique character or personality that each of us was is no more. It has flickered out like a fire in a fireplace. There is nothing of it left for a heaven or a hell. There is no space or time for eternal and detachable soul, and there must not be any more space or time for the dogma that occasions it. This guiding force we call life simply pervades every corner or fiber of our bodies.

THE CHANGING SELF

In an earlier state of evolutionary development, where imagination and complex or abstract thinking had not yet had their day, the power of the brain was essentially used to orchestrate and facilitate basic physical and social functioning. This development continues. Presently, and comparatively speaking, the human brain provides us with the capacity to do much more, including all those pursuits that have no other purpose other than self-enrichment. For we humans there are a myriad of ideas, thoughts, feelings, emotions, beliefs and opinions that we can now entertain, nurture, or live by. An idea can be programmed into a person's mind, as typically happens with children. Also, an idea can simply be accepted by a person on blind faith or trust. An idea can also be learned. By learn I mean applying one self to the rigorous process of weighing and comparing ideas and thereby acquiring knowledge or gaining new insights. Learning is more challenging than the other ways. It requires discipline, work, and stamina. The great satisfaction is that at least the idea is yours; you have earned it. It is accompanied by a feeling of growth and development. Change is no longer a demon.

Leibniz believed that our ideas are innate and must then be extracted from within. However, Locke believed that our ideas are received from external sources and then processed within. Actual learning encompasses both of these approaches. Both require hard work, study, and application to the task. On the other hand, a young child or prospective learner does not have any real choice as to what ideas he or she will possess. Simply put, a young child, in the truest sense of the word, is programmed. Those closest to a child are of course the primary programmers. Depending on the child's circumstances some combination of parents, families, churches, schools, television, and the Internet will do this for him. Not all ideas programmed into our youth are crucial ones. But some are. Ideas about how to live life, about how to view the world, and about how to view oneself are fundamental. These are important because, these first fundamental ideas on any given subject do become who and what we are. Since who, what, and how a person is, is dictated by the very ideas and notions that constitute our cerebral or "mental" processes, those first fundamental ideas that are programmed into us become enormously critical. Whether those ideas were originally the product of reason, fact, and experience or whether they are essentially dogma based becomes decisive. These persons who are bound and confined by dogma have virtually no chance to fully develop their thinking in the particular area that is at issue.

Some programmed ideas are actually based on real thinking, fact, or experience. These can still be very difficult to overcome even when a better thinking is proffered, but the possibility for change is present. But when the idea to be changed is essentially dogmatic there is virtually no chance for change. Dogma, not being based on reason and fact, is impenetrable by reasoning and experience. Only reasoned ideas are susceptible to reasoned alternatives. Dogma to the dogmatist is superior to all else. Against dogma, all else must succumb, and that includes reason, logic, fact, and experience. These earliest of ideas become so deeply rooted that it is virtually impossible to eradicate them. The expression we are what we eat contains elements of truth. The notion that we are our ideas, that we are what we think and we are what we believe, contains an even greater truth.

Human beings tend to have exaggerated views about their ability to reason or think. Actually, we deal with most matters by just parroting what we have learned from others. What we parrot is not self-produced but borrowed at fair market value. We feel that we think a lot more than we really do. Even if we do think a lot, most of us rarely question the basic or core ideas about how our world is organized or if the world is really working well. As we discussed earlier, we are our ideas and our earliest ideas do not relinquish their favored positions readily. So when we question core ideals, (political, economic and religious ones), especially those already dogmatically based, we do so with a brain that is already the seat of those very dogmatic ideals. To find fault with our core values, then, would be tantamount to finding grave fault with ourselves. To relinquish old core values with new ones is tantamount to re-creating ourselves. And we all know that we should not mess with perfection.

The dynamic in play here is that the very mind that is making judgments with regard to the value of new ideas does so by using the ideas and views already possessed and doing so as though they were the proper measure. Potential new ideas are judged and weighed by the very ideas that will be replaced if the new ideas win out. When the already possessed ideas are dogmatic there is no hope for change. If the already possessed ideas are the product of reason and experience there is some hope but not a lot. Attempting to get beyond ourselves will be a formidable challenge for human beings for a very long period of time. When dogma is the foundation for old views the problem is exacerbated. That is because the primary tool for change is reason and reason has little or no chance against sacred belief, whether religious or secular. This has always contributed to the degree by which we can be manipulated and the intractable nature of the status quo and to the near impossibility of achieving needed change. The inordinately wealthy, the clergy, pseudo democrats, and nondemocrats of the world have relied on this narrow human cerebral nature to help them control and manipulate everyone else. It is always these powerful pillars and respected members of the community who beat this drum of the status quo the loudest. If we are everywhere in chains, as Rousseau once noted, it is by the chains of this natural but limiting myopia and the dogma that it so readily covets.

Chapter Two

Religion and God

The Disconnect between Religion and God

In confronting the ills of the world, one problem is the self. As we saw in the previous chapter, we need to confront our own physicality and overcome our complex dynamic with institutions and traditions in order to think clearly about solutions to the world's problems. Because we both make these institutions and are made *by* them, finding a way through the scaffold of our received dogma to think in ways that are shaped by reason and experience, rather than custom and tradition, is a challenge. IN ORDER TO TRANSFORM ONE SELF WITHIN THE CONTEXT OF RELIGIOUS BELIEF, ONE MUST CHANGE HIS OR HER OWN IDEAS ABOUT RELIGION AND GOD.

How can it be that religious belief is one of the problems and not one of the solutions? The short answer is that religious dogma is still dogma and therefore it is fraught with the same evils that we recognize in secular dogmas. The longer answer involves a critical analysis of just what religion is, what it does, and how it does it. To this end our first task is to carefully separate and distinguish the notion of god from that of religion. God or the notion of god can stand on its own and is not, in any respect, dependent on religious belief. One's conclusion that there is a god, or that there might be a god, can and should be reached totally independently from religious belief. This is so because to link or include the notion of god with religious belief makes dogmatic man god's maker.

Theism, a belief in god, entails a firm conviction or affirmation of the mind that god is real and has existence. *Religion,* on the other hand, is an adherence to scriptures, theological dogma, and tradition. With this in mind, we see that theists and atheists can each be divided into two groups. Theists can be divided into religious and nonreligious theists. Although a theist is one who necessarily believes in god, not all theists attach religious scripture to their belief in god. The belief of a nonreligious theist is an unencumbered view that there is a god or causal agent that is responsible for our being and continued existence. Because there is no religion attached to this belief in god, the notion of god remains for the theist a belief based on a secularized and reasoned necessity. This secular god perhaps, once having created the universe or the stuff of the universe, allows the natural procession of life in all its aspects to simply unfold. With belief in a secular god, man's daily ethical, moral, and social dilemmas are left to humans themselves for resolution. As this god is the author of the natural world there would seem to be no place for supernatural interventions, miracles, or promises of eternal salvation.

To a religious theist thinking of god outside the context of religious scripture and tradition is impossible. This is because both are learned simultaneously and they each hold up the other. Without an omniscient god, religious belief would be insufficiently frightful and compelling so as to garner fear and blind loyalty. Without religious belief there would be no need for a personal god or fountainhead from whom issue dire admonitions and commands. Without religious belief there is no religious god. Without religious god there is no religious belief. Only the religious theist finds the interconnectedness of religion and god to be real.

For the nonreligious theist and of course the atheist there is no inherent or legitimate connection between god and religion. It is here where religious man finds himself in the precarious but revealing position of perhaps having created his god and not the other way around. The natural wonderment that fills the heart of the secular theist becomes the dogmatic certainty in the mind of the religious theist. The fact remains they are both theists.

Atheists, too, come in two types. The first is someone who simply does not have the conviction that god exists. The second is someone who actively believes that there is no god. This atheist is not a mere nonbeliever. He adds to his nonbelief an active affirmative disbelief. He knows that there is no god just as clearly as a believer knows that there is a god. To nonbelievers of the first type, this complete confidence of both believers and active disbelievers is difficult to understand. Their confidence does not seem to be curtailed by the profoundly limited nature of the mental and intuitive processes of the human organism. The nonbeliever, or agnostic, understands his limits and his ignorance and acknowledges that there are some things that we as human beings can never know. He appreciates, however, that the notion of a possible god is the reasoned outgrowth of wondering and contemplating how it is that we are here and experiencing life.

Belief is something active and affirmative. It is not passive or equivocal. To be a theist requires that one hold an active affirmative view about god's existence. If it is not clearly and unmistakably held, then it is not belief. And this is exactly where atheists and nontheists find themselves. They lack this affirmative belief in god. Therefore, if one is equivocal about god's existence one is necessarily atheistic—without a belief in god. Looking at it this way, as either the presence or absence of belief, there is no trinity of theists, atheists, and agnostics. When it comes to belief in god there are only atheists or theists. If you are agnostic, your agnosticism necessarily defines you as a nonbeliever or atheist.

The question whether god exists, however intriguing it might be, for our purposes is and should be of limited concern. Its irrelevance is based on several facts. First, even if the universe was actually created by god, this truth will never be revealed by the mind of any earthly creature. It is true that great thinkers throughout history have attempted to prove or disprove god's existence, but human mental processes are simply not adequate to do so. We cannot just think our way to all truths. All these philosophers and theologians could do was to put forth their best arguments as to the likelihood of god's existence. Such ontological arguments for god's existence have not gone to waste, for even to this day such arguments are used by theists to support or justify their already held religious views. Logic does permit us to follow certain lines of thought that are more persuasive than other manners of thought. But it is thought itself that is deficient. In his *Tractatus Logico-Philosophicus* of 1921, Ludwig Wittgenstein wrote, "The limits of my language mean the limits of my world. . . . Logic pervades the world: the limits of the world are also its limits. . . . We cannot think what we cannot think: so what we cannot think we cannot say either. . . . What we cannot speak about we must pass over in silence." God is clearly one of those things that we must "pass over in silence" because no matter how completely science ultimately describes and explains the natural world, it will never be able to elucidate the ultimate metaphysical mystery of how and why there is the stuff of the natural world.

Second, if we assume *arguendo* that a causal and sustaining god is real, it is clear that the natural order of things was put in motion long before the appearance of humans and will undoubtedly continue long after our demise. History and prehistory have given us no reason to expect that this will not remain the case. Without an understandable purpose, at least to humans, the world moves on and on. We abide by the rules, the realities, and parameters of existence that this god would have set for us and we do so without any thought of unexpected exceptions to them. With or without god, life for us remains the same. We deal with the demands of each day by doing the best we can solely with the natural faculties at our disposal. To actually know that there is a god would provide us with no greater advantage or purpose. If we actually knew that there was a god, that would necessitate that we were of another order of being. It would require that we were more than the earthly physical creatures that we are. However, if we were as we are and somehow we were aware of god's existence, it would still change nothing—except for giving us the realization that this god had every intention that we get by with what he originally and naturally gave us. There would be no room for intermittent supernatural revelations and miracles. We would still be left with navigating through the same physical world with the same physical attributes and without any additional purpose. And we would still know that it is not for us to know why and for what purpose we exist. Based on our past experience we justifiably continue to anticipate that the present reality will remain as it is for all of our succeeding days. This view does not necessitate a dismal outlook. The reverse is true. Reality and truth are not our enemies. We must understand that it is solely this earthly life that provides us with joy and love as well as sorrow and pain. To continue to deny this truth is to continue to deny reality. When our species' run is over, it will be over, god or no god. So if there is a god what better way to show respect and appreciation to it than by fully utilizing all of our endowments as human beings as we exist in the world it has made us a part of. To show dissatisfaction with ourselves and with this world and to anticipate and expect a better one in the future is to show disrespect and arrogance. And if there is no god what better way to show respect for ourselves as a part of nature than to fully utilize all that we somehow possess and to appreciate life as it is.

For all people, life goes on without change and with all the natural boundaries and constraints pre-set. Religious belief is man's own attempt to change these boundaries of life, to change the rules and realities of existence. Through religious dogma humans mysteriously but effectively become their own god. For the price of "your" soul you receive the promise of eternal soul, a promise to make you eternal. This gift of eternity requires as quid pro quo undying devotion and fealty to religious scripture. This nonlife on earth is deemed preparatory for real and eternal existence rather than an intrinsically precious opportunity to be.

A different reality acknowledges that as human beings we are endowed with bodies, containing brains and all the other tools of life. This is what we have; this is what we are. There is nothing more. There will never be anything more. A possible real god has given us nothing more to work with or to work for. This is our fate—and our blessing.

God, if real, would dwarf the human-made gods of religious belief with their all too narrow and petty concerns. The idea that a possible real god would share with only a few select persons a variety of narrow and static rules for the world to live by when such dogmas undermine the natural bodily tools of instinct and reason is too contradictory to be taken seriously. This would require that the chimerical communications to a very select few are to be seriously taken by the rest of humankind as the basis for what is worthy, meaningful, and real in the universe. Our entire species would have to forgo that which is apparent, clear, and natural. The human nature in each of us would have to be abandoned so that we could continue to be loyal members of Nietzsche's herd. We would forever have to live in the darkness of Plato's cave. We would forever have to fear ourselves and our possibilities and accept as true that which we are told. The last thing god would need is religious belief muddying-up the clear waters of life.

The fact is that religion has stolen or appropriated for its own use the notion of god. Religions invent their own gods, giving to each god its own prized psyche, endowing god with the values the religion upholds, making god in the image of the humans who create him. This false image of god is the very heart of religious belief and should not be allowed to stand. What really separates human beings from other animals is our ability to change and develop ourselves intellectually and ethically. But religion demands acceptance of its static teachings with blind faith. Religious belief maps out areas where human inquiry is off-limits. To religion real growth and development outside the straitjacket of its own dogma is nothing less than seditious. Religion's program has been quite the opposite. What could have been worse for our species than to be told never to use our brain's beyond first gear; or, to be told to distrust our bodily nature for it is to be controlled and overcome. What could have been worse than for a person to have been taught that one's body is a temporary earthly prison and that this body is not the lone means to experience life and self. This type of programming results in a distortion of existence and is nothing less than crippling to natural human growth and happiness. In place of attaining a sense of self-worth through body, one is told to deny, distrust, disarm, and disown it. Stale and static religious law cannot bear the light of day.

THE TAKING IN OF LIFE

Methodically, mechanically, and always meticulously following certain unchanging and obligatory rules, the world proceeds, convulsing and then calming in the greatest harmony imaginable. As though it had been wound like a clock, the universe, our world, proceeds in its relentless and undaunted manner seemingly without purpose and seemingly indifferent to us. The universe in its perpetual winding, clinging, and repelling ways seems to be saying confidently but almost inaudibly "for man there is nothing more." And as its last bit of advice it admonishes us that whether we accept or reject this humanly incomprehensible happening called universe as sufficient or insufficient for humanity's purposes is of no account to it. The universe does not require people but we require it.

We human beings, when considering the universe and the world at large, do not seem to concern ourselves much with the absence of some apparent or demonstrable end or purpose to the universe's boundless activity. It is quite a different thing, however, when we direct our attention to ourselves. We forget that we are but a part of the natural scheme. Its continual and seemingly pointless procession of activity and life is insufficient for our regal and elevated tastes. Through religious dogma we are assured that we are better than and above the very universe, the very world, that we are generated from and that enables us to be. But reason, real thinking, tells us that without the universe, without the earth, there is no human experience. Through religious programming, however, we have been led to believe that there is a great end or design for us in a better and more fitting world. To those who are religious, this temporal and temporary earthly residence must surely account for more than mere being and doing. But when being and doing are discounted, life itself is discounted. And so, as a result of this religious programming, the sweetness and light of existence itself is lost.

Normally in the life of individual human beings specific goals are identified, considered, and perhaps pursued. Most of us find that a goal-oriented life is both helpful and profitable. It is helpful in that it directs our interests, energies, and abilities jointly toward a fruitful path. It is profitable because it often results in the attainment of satisfying achievements. Educational, material, financial, and social accomplishments are important, if not necessary, to a good life. However, the journey to success, or failure for that matter, is where life is awakened in us and where it is felt fiber by fiber. It is the process of giving an endeavor whatever one can bring to bear on it such that it makes "now" so vividly real. In other animals daily life is more instinctive but still purposeful. But for all animals, including us, the point of life ought to be in the engaging in and reveling in existence itself. Although goals may become important aspects of one's life they are only the forms of life. They in themselves do not constitute life. They are important pragmatic signposts within one's life but they are not the point of life.

The goal of individual human life must involve the heightened taking in of life itself. That is to truly partake in it and not just go through the motions of life. Life is truly felt in the intense engagement with the natural world and the life conditions that transform the quietude of our bodies into uncontrollable and personally revealing clusters of emotions and impressions. Doing and being become their own rewards and are nature's true gift of life. Failure to know and enjoy the warmth and glow of being, of existence itself, is to miss out on life itself.

For those in the trap of religious dogma, the world is insufficient for humanity's high purposes. Therefore, they miss out on the glory and rewarding nature of our world, and all that is natural becomes foreign and suspect. They no longer can bear the fact that we are part and parcel, brothers and sisters, with the natural world. Skin and bones, eyes and nose, drinking and eating are all unpleasant reminders of our physical natural being. Those caught in religious dogma feel that they must live forever, dining and dancing at the footsteps of god himself. They foolishly disrobe themselves of their physical earthly being and attire themselves in the lofty loneliness of a happy tomorrow that will never come. The sad irony of this is that if the earth and universe are not good enough for us, we are not good enough for each other either.

GOD EXPROPRIATED

Although the question of god's existence can never be answered and, in the end, is not relevant to our daily lives, this does not mean that god's presence should not be contemplated or that we should not venture into areas where only wonderment can properly reside.

We perhaps engage in such matters because we can and because we like to flirt with grand ideas that resemble answers. Engaging in the realm of the metaphysical is therefore not always to be scorned from an intellectual point of view as long as it is remembered that such endeavors are speculations about matters that are a step or two beyond reason's reach. Those who are intellectually honest, however, will admit that what they are left with in the end is not knowledge or truth but simply opinion and speculation.

These opinions cannot be arrived at through reason. So what, in the final analysis, is their source? We all have preferences and personal biases that will form the nature of the universe that we find most likely or appealing. But those who are bound by religious dogma, perhaps too vain to admit that they can only opine on the subject, take refuge in a third category: belief. Whereas opinions and knowledge are generally seen as the direct result of our own reasoning, belief is the product of trusting the espoused views or words of another person as the truth without the need for reliable evidence or sound argument. For those who embrace religious dogma, belief in god carries more weight than mere opinion about god. And when dealing with matters that cannot be refuted, such as god's existence, belief is seen as more durable and worthy than mere opinion. Belief in god, being irrefutable, is not answerable to anyone or anything.

Those who embrace belief ultimately contribute to a powerful and horrendous fiction: that god and religion are identical, that religion is the only path to god. There is no logical or experiential path from religion to god, but we get there because we are raised to believe in the link. It is apparent that we never do get from point A to point B. We are essentially placed at point B at the outset. Point B becomes our starting point and not our destination. We never have to make the connection between god and religion because that is done for us by immediate and continuous indoctrination at the earliest possible age. Maturity and reflection never have a chance to weigh in on the matter. They are bypassed. For the manipulator this is crucial as it eliminates all competition. This is why Ignatius of Loyola was confident that if you brought him your son by the age of eight your son would be his forever. Most human beings, once having been taught something of importance at an early age, and then having it reinforced throughout their lives, find it almost impossible to ever not believe it.

The reason why received dogma is so influential is that we are our ideas; the ideas that dwell in our minds truly constitute who and what we are. Beyond biology our personalities and our psychics are the cumulative result of the earliest experiences and thoughts that do make us what and who we are. To replace earlier programmed religious ideas, then, is to actually modify who and what we are. This phenomenon occurs without regard to the substance of the programmed matter. The content of any dogma, including religious scripture, may be of importance but is a separate matter and not necessarily relevant to why it becomes so difficult for persons to get beyond said dogma. To think about god in a secular fashion would be quite foreign to a religiously raised person. As we saw in the previous chapter, change in the self is a profound happening and is usually avoided. Most religious persons, even through their adult life, find it more comfortable and less scary to just continue to believe. It remains, however, that belief is a one-way ticket from reality and real existence to the world of make-believe. Very few people have the intellectual honesty and the moral courage to change, even in the light of displayed maturity in other areas of life and thought. The sad irony is that the ability to change or modify who and what we are is perhaps what primarily separates us from other animals.

A further byproduct of this mental misdirection is that god, the possible real god, is reduced by religion to the size and shape of the religious person's mental straitjacket. God, supposedly the maker of all things, is contorted and squeezed into human perspective and vision. From the possibility of a real god, we end up with a fictional religious idol. The real god would have created humans. The religious person, however, creates religious god, his own god. All the concerns that seem to consume the religious person now consume the religious god. This contrived creator of the universe now seems to be concerned about little else other than daily human conduct and behavior. The religious person likewise manufactures heavens, souls, and eternities for man. He simultaneously reduces earthly existence to a demeaning and shameful episode, expropriating god's possibility and reducing human endowments to sinister inclinations. This legacy has done nothing short of robbing individuals of much of their personal existence.

FAITH

Another distortion that emerges from religious dogma is the prejudice against those who are not theists. It is a common view that those without religious faith are suspect, not to be trusted, or even an enemy of god. The holding of religious faith of at least some kind is a requirement for many kinds of participation in our society, for example running for major political office. Having religious faith of some kind entitles a person to some minimum level of respect and legitimacy.

The idea that someone who does not believe in god is a threat to religion is curious. How can religion be viewed as fragile when it has been around in some form for thousands of years? It is because for those same thousands of years religious institutions have done literally everything in their power to successfully maintain their positions depending on the times, locations, and circumstances involved. If one's institutions are truly worthy and therefore largely self-sustaining, this constant bombardment of propaganda and programming and the perennial reliance on political, economic, and military power would not be required.

Why is it that people of religious faith feel that it is so crucial that everyone else have a religious faith of some sort? Disagreements and inconsistencies among religious dogmas do not threaten the foundation of any of those dogmas because the foundation for all religious dogma is the same: blind faith, involuntarily acquired at childhood and then reinforced by repetition and ritual throughout one's life. Because the differences among dogmas are only as to doctrine, and not to the legitimacy of dogma itself, religious dogmatists can coexist, even though with some uneasiness. But nondogmatic theists and atheists challenge the idea of dogma itself. They imply that the institutions and traditions we have inherited and relied on throughout our lives are based upon make-believe and are unbecoming of contemporary human beings. The nontheist represents a personal challenge to, and an assault upon, the very make-up of those who believe. It challenges their understanding of who they are, what their purpose on earth is, how he should behave, and what they can expect after death. Nontheists represent a profound challenge to the fundamental bases of the lives of religious people and the beliefs that were implanted in them at an early age. This holds true for those who have been born again as well as those who change religions; although the particulars of faith may have changed for them, their reliance on religious dogma is intact.

Religious faith is not the product of life experiences, common sense, or mature thought. Religious belief thrives best in an unthinking and uncritical world. Sensing this, religious persons of all faiths feel more at home in a world of dogma. For a religious person to deal with another religious person, even of a different faith, who appreciates the blind basis of religious faith is one thing. They share the same dual reality of both impenetrability and vulnerability. Impenetrable because they do not have to defend their views in a normal manner upon any basis of common experience or common sense. Vulnerable because of this same awareness, that thought and experience are not only unnecessary for their blind belief but antagonistic toward it. The punishment for questioning this blind faith within the religious community is the charge of blasphemy itself. Religious persons know, however, that nonreligious persons enjoy an absolute immunity from such a charge. Hence, we find the natural reluctance in the religious person to deal on a multiple of levels with those who are free of dogma. What threatens the world of religious dogma most is nondoctrinaire education and openness of thought.

Those who are not religious endure their share of sorrow and heartbreak in life. However, they deal with them in a realistic manner and as a natural aspect of life itself and not as a product of divine will or retribution. It is because of this that the secular person will grow, develop, mature, and relish—with discernment and discrimination—both the pleasant and not-so-pleasant aspects of engagement with life itself. To go through an entire life with the belief that you are not fully adequate and sufficient to deal with all that can occur in life is truly a cross to bear. To be sure, life can become quite miserable. It can cause you to wonder whether it is worth it. But all this despair and anguish can be addressed and dealt with, however imperfectly, by individuals with the help and understanding of others without relying on irrational explanations or justifications, without blaming or assigning fault through supernatural mechanisms. The person of religious faith all too often is left to rely on learned lessons like: god works in mysterious ways; it is not for us to question god's will; or, accept your fate here on earth because faith will one day get you to a better world. Self-reliance among religious persons becomes partial and is necessarily diminished. The end result is that natural confidence is stifled, and our natural attributes and strengths atrophy. And somewhere along the line the religiously based weaknesses and deficiencies forge a less natural and spontaneous person who is ill equipped to fully enjoy the sweetness and light of life. In actuality, we are strong earthly creatures who can deal with tough earthly difficulties. We do so fully engaged in the life process. Reliance on make-believe is not required or beneficial in the long run. To a serious and mature person the artificial elixir of make-believe can never be an option.

Religious faith is faith in many things except in oneself. Faith in oneself is not arrogance but a deep humility. It is a deep courage that as an earthly being, endowed as one is and not differently, one is built to succeed to the extent that circumstances permit. An opportunity to overcome our surroundings and at times even to overcome ourselves is the stuff from which real life is constituted. Engaging with the world and personally accepting the serious challenges of life, rather than feeling ourselves to be objects at the mercy of circumstances or higher forces, is what makes us alive and what provides us with our substantial rewards. Reliance on religious verse, in the long run, is no more helpful than drugs and alcohol. This does not mean that life will be easy or sorrow free; the tragedies of life are still tragedies. However, personal acceptance of serious challenges is the stuff from which real growth occurs. Becoming distraught as a result of a terrible event is natural. Doing whatever one can to avoid dealing with it, however, is destructive. Instead of religious faith we need to have faith in ourselves; faith that our kind will endure and prosper as dictated by the laws of nature; faith that the natural dynamic that we are a part of will itself endure insofar as permitted by the laws of nature; faith that we will have done that which nature always intended for us to do; faith that our minds can become tools for good and not weapons for bad; faith that the ultimate good for ourselves and the ultimate tribute to a possible real god is that we live each moment while on earth as it was intended to be lived; faith in the face of almost total ignorance, ignorance about why, when, and how we are here; faith based on the realization that we are here and have no choice by our nature but to succeed and to fully express ourselves as we can; and faith too that, whatever the end might be, it is also ours.

A SPECIES MISGUIDED

Because religious belief has expropriated the notion of god, it has been able to profoundly affect humanity's view of itself and society's ability to flourish. Our view of ourselves has become artificial and distorted: denying our flesh and bones, clinging to a self-serving perception that we alone among earthly creatures are special partners with god, blurring the differences between myth and reality. When society is in need of making important adjustments to improve life for its citizens, religious belief can be counted on to attack the rational and the reasonable as dangerous subterfuges for seditious purposes and evil change. When objectivity is needed it injects emotion. When human emotion is needed it asserts cold and brutal directives from above. And all this inhumanity in order to sustain and perpetuate dogma. This constitutes a departure from reality itself into the land of pretend, invention, and distortion. The resultant effects, which are not always readily apparent, have misguided humans over much of recorded history. The continual reliance on a preordained godly and infallible source of truth, right, and correctness is both discouraging and incredibly harmful and debilitating to our species.

Why have human beings turned ourselves over to the myth and make-believe of dogma? Perhaps we were overwhelmed with the implications of our developing intellect and sought to calm our growing uneasiness with magic, superstition, and religion. Perhaps our growing intellect highlighted just how much we didn't understand, and any certainty, however false, was better than the uncertainty of a newly discovered ignorance. As people turned to dogma for a sense of certainty, these beliefs became traditional and were implanted in young people too immature to question them. Once dogma is planted in the mind it is next to impossible to remove. Therefore the rational process, real thinking, takes a second seat. Religious and secular dogmas have always curtailed thought, examination, and exploration. Because of religious belief our real thinking and logical analysis have been thwarted and at times even made to be sinful or dangerous.

As a species, we have an interest in continued natural and healthy evolution and development. Our interests are better served by relying on and utilizing our innate and developing natural ability to critically think than endlessly relying on deadening dogma. Religious and secular dogmas have retarded our ability to further and naturally develop individually and society's ability to successfully nurture a meaningful coexistence among all people. Where dogma begins, thinking and development stops. The relinquishment of the privilege to use our thinking powers and to follow wherever reason and experience take us is a self-thwarting baptism. All dogmas, religious and secular, result in the disuse of an indispensable part of ourselves and the atrophy of one of our most important human attributes—real thinking. Truth and knowledge are acquired, however unevenly, as the result of our applying our thinking powers on various subjects and are not simply received by one generation passing on dogmatic traditions to the next generation.

Religious belief, along with secular dogma, has been a significant contributor to a global environment hostile to respect for and fruitful coexistence among all members of our species. The idea behind religious belief is that you now have correct answers and proper direction for the important issues of life. You need not engage in that difficult and unsettling self-examination that is prerequisite to understanding and appreciating the other person's position. There is no need for a meaningful exchange of ideas among religious people because those ideas they espouse are not really their own. Those ideas have already been established for them by others. For the most part they practice what they have been taught and they are not the makers or definers of said ideas. Because of this there is no room for compromise or accommodation among them. The best they can hope for is nondestructive coexistence among themselves. Outward coexistence among dogmatists of different faiths secretly engenders an uneasy feeling because such outward cooperation involves an insincere togetherness. Imposition of one's own belief system on others remains a latent and sad dream of all religious people just as retention of one's own belief system is patently the prerequisite to that end.

Where dogma prevails, being members of the same species ends up being less important than adhering to one's own closed and complete belief system. Sharing the same humanity does not count for as much as not sharing the same dogmatic beliefs. The appalling and unspeakable acts against other persons that dogmatism condones or requires has been documented throughout history. Even without religion it is a challenge for humans to be fair and just with one another, to accommodate and compromise with our own kind. However, when religious, dogmatic belief is introduced, these challenges become wholly unacceptable accommodations to perceived evil and impurity. Religious belief by its nature separates people. When you seriously hold to a dogma and that dogma is the most important thing in your life, there is little room for others, or the views and needs of others. The superficial peace among religious persons is both shallow and short-lived. Nature on its own does not hinder personal growth or inflame the fires of discord among our numbers. Human nature is inevitably blamed for our inability to get along peaceably and constructively with one another, when in fact it is our acquired social and religious nature that sows the seeds of discord. We, confined by the straight jacket of religious and secular dogma, have accomplished that on our own.

GOD THE VICTIM

A consequence of religious belief is that god is reduced in stature to the level of human mental processes. The thoughts, feelings, and concerns of a religious god are ultimately those of the people who created him. Religious belief is based on scripture that in turn derives its sacred status from revelation and at landmark moments god's personal carnal or bodily appearance. In this communicative process we are supposed to learn of god's concerns and wishes. However, the real dynamic at play here is that humans are literally defining god's intentions and sculpturing god's being. The maker of the universe, and perhaps much more, is contorted and reduced to a power source and legitimizer of those who created him. Behind all the talk of praise and servanthood, religious people exploit the concept of real god with fine-tuned precision and skill. Only blind belief through dogmatic acceptance of make-believe makes this deception a social fact around much of the world. Like all earthly organisms, human beings are limited and restricted. We can only function within the confines of our physical selves. A possible real god can never be understood or appreciated in human terms. The human arrogance that is required to continually put forth this concocted story is perhaps the ultimate "sin." If it were not so serious and hurtful to our species' health and well-being, one could let it be. But it is a malignancy and should not be left to continue. Dogma and dogmatic thought must be seen for what they are and the harm they do. Dogma always functions at the expense of the many. Humans, religious or secular, despite all their desire to do so, cannot begin to conceptualize a real god and can only impute to their religious god their own all-too-human attributes. Religious god is dependent, characteristic by characteristic, on religious people's particular predilections. This is why religious god is so concerned with every little detail of each of our lives. And religious detail turns quickly into religious control, the source of so much misery.

Those with religious belief create god in their own image. Just as distorting, they elevate themselves to a quasi-godly status. After all, in their view, god has singularly selected humanity above all other earthly creatures for special standing. Humans are not just superior to other creatures but are a qualitatively different kind of being. This belief flows from humans' belief that we and we alone have the power to be moral or immoral. Only we have that extra mental capacity to actually make decisions that can at times override instinct or habit. It is this extra mental capacity that gives man greater freedom than other creatures and, of course, at times gives him much greater grief. Those who are religious sum up this extra mental flexibility as free will stemming directly from the soul. They expropriate a natural physical human function and recycle it as eternal detachable soul. It is this that puts him at god's side, that dogmatically elevates man to the heavens. Possessing unique qualities or attributes like a supernatural soul or spirit, humans truly must be supernatural themselves. Our vanity and arrogance come ever so close to mimicking the half-men half-gods of ancient lore. This psychological orientation is so well ingrained that it actually hurts those with religious belief to think of themselves as animals, despite the fact that we are part of the food chain, share similar body parts with any number of other animals, and have a 96% overlap in our DNA with certain chimpanzees. The mental slumber demanded by dogma serves religious people well by numbing their senses to their own physical reality and the physical reality around them.

PROGRAMMED FOREVER

By any rational criteria the claims of religion are fantastic and fanciful. They defy common experience and common sense. Religious views cannot be proved or disproved; they are beyond attack and doubt, a weakness that, for dogmatists, is their most alluring strength. It sets the ground work for magic, miracles, and revelation. These in turn provide sufficient proof of truth and sufficient footing for the sacred. Belief's unassailable nature will work only if the blind trust in dogma is programmed into a youthful mind before exposure to any other competing ideas that are based on reason or experience. Religious man wears a special pride in owning this special belief about the ultimate power behind the universe and the nature and pureness of the world beyond. To a healthy adult such claims should only find a home in the realm of make-believe. But religious dogma is exempt from normal human scrutiny and criticisms that most other areas of thought and action must survive. If similar fantastic claims were made about any matter outside the domain of religious teachings and thought, the claimants would be dismissed as mentally suspect. So how is it that so many people throughout the world still profess religious beliefs of one sort or another?

The answer requires a basic appreciation for how the human organism works based on the best evidence available to us. The fact of the matter is, as noted before, we are our ideas. Ideas in this sense encompass thoughts, impressions, experiences and all the rest of mental activity. It is crucial to understand that there is no secret center or homunculus that embodies the permanent real you and is the you that experiences life. In fact there is no separation or distinction between the you that experiences life and the life experience itself. The you that experiences is the experience. The experiencing that is going on in and about you is going on by virtue of the body and the mental processes it produces being in a harmonious conjunction with one another. Character and personality are the end products of bodily activity and mental processes, and without bodily activity, as when body is dead, there is no character or personality or individual human. Hence, to replace an old idea with a new one is like replacing a part of you with a new part of you.

Modification and change are personal to the core. To change is to leave behind a part of one's self. To put part of one's self behind to make room for a new part is profound—it is an admission of previous imperfection. One needs to place a high value on truth and maturity in order to face such a change. It requires a rare courage. This is why the first ideas that find a home in our minds almost always endure and end up permanently determining who and what we are. Our personalities and our identities are the cumulative and combined result of these earliest ideas. This is why it is crucial to religion that its ideas be implanted in its subjects at an early age. To replace our earliest ideas with new and different ideas is to actually destroy what we were and to become something new. This process of self-change is a dramatic event of the first order. Even a slight change in our daily lives is somewhat difficult for most of us; fundamental change is almost impossible to accomplish. And because change inevitably has implications not only for the individual but for the community, such change is discouraged by society in a myriad of ways. Such is the power of the childhood-learned dogma supported and reinforced by a panoply of relentless societal institutions and sanctions.

THE ONE-TWO PUNCH

In order for religious doctrine to be an attractive and viable product, two elements must be present simultaneously. First, religious doctrine must profess and convince us that we are somehow flawed and in need of serious assistance. Second, it must profess and convince us that it has the answer to our shortcomings or weaknesses. Neither of these can succeed without the other; you do not need crutches if you can walk without them.

All religious dogmas must by their nature reflect grave concern over some perceived problem or problems. For religious dogma it is the inadequacy of the human being that is the concern, an inadequacy or deficiency that begins at birth and remains a lifelong flaw. Even helpless infants are deficient and evil-laden and require cleansing and purification. This, ironically, makes of god a shoddy workman. It is as though religious belief is needed to complete the job that god did not finish. God gives us abilities and attributes that enable us to successfully navigate through life, but religious belief tells us god must have inadvertently left something out. There must have been some kind of oversight on his part. His human creations are not self-sufficient on their own but weak, evil, and not up to the challenge on their own. Their bodies and minds are a curse. Their earthly home is a horrific obstacle course. Their decision-making deficient and their nature bad.

Through the miracle of revelation, however, certain special people are anointed by god to tell the rest of us religious prescriptions can make up for our inadequate and deficient human attributes. Humans become the prey of their own manufactured myths, creating both the problem and alleged solution. Our natural strength, alertness, and instincts have no place in our lives other than as tumor-like symptoms that must be eliminated or held in abeyance. Our bodies and minds then become objects of scorn and distrust. Existence becomes a tightrope where each precarious step must be taken in strict accordance with the demands of religion's own particular physics. One can navigate through life's labyrinth of pitfalls only by meticulously following religious scripture. This lifelong shame bequeathed to us by religious belief is exceeded only by the threat of eternal hell and the scorn from god himself. And whatever you do, do not rely on yourself. The demeaning nature of this artificially contrived ordeal is nothing less than catastrophic to the individual human being.

FEED ME

Among the many problems with religious faith or dogma is that it is not self-sustaining. This is because it does not appeal to our natural selves. It must be continually fed or it will starve. Left alone without continual dogmatic reinforcement, the individual would gradually and naturally begin to apply more and more of his mental faculties to the problems of the day. Figuring out a solution for oneself is quite different from seeking the answer from a book of answers. The former requires utilization of ourselves and the latter requires only appealing to an outside source. For dogma to flourish, constantly reinforcing dogmatic teachings and beliefs is mandatory and requires the full complement of institutional techniques. Through dogma, our cerebral processes remain underused and distracted from their natural rhythm and flow. Understandably the brain reacts uncomfortably to dogma because the brain needs to work in its natural way, accumulating ideas and then weighing and comparing them and then dropping or adding more ideas. In this way growth occurs.

Religious dogma or faith cannot accommodate this evaluative process. This process is in fact a threat to it. All dogma requires is that its ideas, truths, and wisdom be accepted in their prepackaged state from only one pre-existing source. Dogma is a great sleeping pill for the mind. To the extent you put the mind to sleep you put the world to sleep. You cannot engage the world in all its dimensions and wonderment through dogmatic directives. Actual and real thinking, the only real engagement with the world around us, is life. There are no shortcuts. Turn off the mind and you turn off much more. Mental processes in their totality are how we meaningfully become a part of the world. Reliance on dogma may be the key to other worlds but not to the world we live in and are a part of. With dogma there is nothing left to uncover or discover. This is true of secular dogmas as well.

Since dogma is unnatural and does not have the capacity to grow, it must constantly be fed by repetition and artistry. To sustain dogma everything in life is interpreted so as to fit the particular dogma. Realty must conform to dogma. Reality conforms to dogma when one through self-deception interprets an event so as to fit into the requirements of dogmatic scripture. Such interpretation occurs without logic, feeling, common sense, or mental well-being. Some level of objectivity can be attained by thinking people. This imperfect objectivity is what humans can do. Dogma removes the need and desire to have to do so. Dogmatists are content with their static and familiar world. It appeals to nothing wholesome, just to inexperience, fears, and weakness. Religious dogmas, as well as secular dogmas, cannot stand up to objectivity, honesty, and maturity.

As a consequence of religious belief, earth becomes burdensome earth. The planet and everything about it are barely suitable, and believers are just thankful that their stay on earth is only temporary and that better accommodations await. They can also be thankful that they will one day shed their animal bodies and all that they entail. And somewhere along this path of self-deception they disconnect with themselves as well as the natural world they were meant to be a part of. To those with religious belief, the world is simply a random testing place that human beings happen to find themselves at. We could have just as well ended up anywhere else. For them our life holds out no immediate, personal, or intimate relationship with the world; there are humans and then there is the rest of the world. We are not of it or with it or an aspect of it. We do not function in concert with it. We are above it. There is no understanding of our oneness with the world or the completeness of that oneness. And there is of course absolutely no understanding of the finality of our life within the context of the universe's continual progression. Dogma does not fit into the universe and the universe does not fit into dogma.

What is important to natural real people is unimportant to fictitious-minded religious people. They live in an artificial world created by themselves and not in the real and natural world created for them. They are always longing for a better and different kind of world and become incapable of truly and completely experiencing the joy of earthly existence. Humans, being unconditionally a part of nature, must bask in nature in order to fully experience life. To do otherwise is self-denial, self-destruction. The real earth, possibly created by a real god, might be risky, problematic, and uncertain; but it is real, and as we are of it we are also equally real.

MORALITY AND RELIGION

Many people doubt the divine basis of religious scripture but still find a basis for supporting religious institutions because those institutions and scriptures constitute the basic source of our morality. They mistakenly believe that without the presence of religious belief, there would be a moral vacuum in society. They see, in the absence of religion, wild uncontrolled sexual, violent, and criminal behavior running rampant. Once again religious belief is guilty of expropriation, this time not of god but of morality as its very own unique possession.

What is morality? Your desk dictionary will probably define moral as pertaining or relating to principles of right or wrong behavior. Morality goes well beyond civil or criminal law. Morality does not depend upon likely or immediate sanctions. It pertains to a person having a sense of what is appropriate behavior under a given set of circumstances. Morality is thought of as being sufficiently ingrained in one's character or mind so as to affect one's conscience. Morality is personal acceptance and compliance with what society holds to be valuable rules or ideas about the correct or appropriate way to think and act as a responsible member of society. What "society holds" makes reference to the virtual universal assent among societal members as to what constitutes appropriate or inappropriate behavior. It is about the sharing together of these values by almost all members of society almost all the time. Imagining a society composed of members who do not share these values would be imagining not so much a society but a chaotic and destructive group of people. Society cannot coexist with chaos and anarchy.

A fundamental precondition to enduring society is morality, through shared custom and tradition. As we will see in chapter 4, morality is not the only precondition to organized and constructive society. Morality is also a necessary consequence of society itself. It is the direct result of successful group formation and functioning.

Morality's absence would in itself prevent serious societal formation and continued existence. As a constituent element of societal physics, morality is no more a choice than circle is to a tire. It is a necessary byproduct of people coming together and functioning as a whole for some period of time. Morality, ethics, mores, customs, and traditions are all natural social phenomena. Morality was not invented or created by religion or religious thinkers. Religious moral doctrines are borrowed from previously existing cultures or times and then repackaged as if they were their very own. Once again religious dogma expropriates what is humanity's by nature. Societies do not need religious belief for there to be morality, structure, and cooperation.

SOUL

The term *soul*, religious man's bridge to the supernatural, has been used ambiguously and misleadingly by philosophers, theologians, and many others when referring to a variety of very human attributes. Over the centuries the words *soul*, *mind*, *core,* and *spirit* have been used interchangeably. Soul has been used as a synonym for feeling, reasoning, and thinking. It has been used to capture the physical phenomena of emotion and exhilaration; the very animating force that we associate with life itself; the thing that gives each of us our individual personhood and character. Soul has been used to refer to that thing in us that permits us to dream, wonder, and appreciate those things that we as humans cannot truly understand. It has been used to refer to that ethical and moral component of man's character, of humans' finest and most elevated self, that purest self that is apart from and above body and earth.

Virtually all things that are good and that separate us from "lower" forms of animals and living creatures are attributed to the human soul. Even presently much of what is deemed good and wonderful and has not yet been fully explained by science is deemed soul. The word *soul* has been used so long in so many ways that for practical purposes it has no significance other than as a dogmatic disguise. This disguise is crucial to perpetuating the notion of continued and eternal existence after death. Without this murky word there would be nothing left of us, after death, to go to heaven or hell. Without this crafty word religious scripture could not promise eternal anything. Without this meaningless word we would all have to deal with life on earth and only life on earth. It gets us out of our bodies and enables us to travel to other worlds. It is our escape mechanism out of our selves and into an eternal nonhuman reality. We leave our humanity and enter into the realm of god's divinity. Not bad for an earthly creature. Through this truly meaningless term, religion fraudulently becomes responsible for and the keeper of virtually all that constitutes our humanity.

We should now realize that everything is body, physical body. We are our bodies and our bodies are us. The entire world of mind and thought is really an aspect of one's physical self. Every idea, thought, or emotion is simply an activity of body. It is our body's systems that dream, create, and wonder. Consciousness and life itself are physical forces involved in incredibly intricate motion. This oscillatory motion of particles is the full substance of consciousness and life. There is no detachable supernatural soul component or ignition to consciousness and life. Consciousness and life are not experienced by a separate entity called soul but together jointly constitute the self. Any dependency that self has is as an aspect of the real world it is a part of and no other. There is nothing else close by that brings life and consciousness to the body. There is nothing else of an ethereal, intangible, or unearthly nature that gives us life or experiences life for us. Life and consciousness are as much a part of nature as are the growth and decay of plants, mountains, and trees. With due respect for Descartes, the idea of a separate mental aspect and a separate physical aspect to each human being is artificial. They are gloriously one and the same. The notion of soul is in the end revealed to be just another method of expropriation by religion.

Religious belief pulls our humanity away from us surreptitiously and then boasts in giving it back under a disguised appearance as something different. Through the use of the term *soul*, it sells back to us what was already ours, our humanity, our natural, physical humanity. Soul is a fraudulent label for concealing what was ours to begin with. Tragically, religion has convinced most of humankind throughout the ages that the animating force of life is something separate and apart from our bodies and the world we live in. And of course the eternal separation that will hopefully take place is totally dependent upon soul and proper religious fealty.

Soul, that thing that makes us special in the eyes of religious god, is in the end just as nonexistent as the religious god. It is a word that erroneously takes credit for body parts and body functions that are natural and real. It tries to give them some supranatural aura that can justify religious misappropriation of what is quite natural and of this world. Some people talk about a religious instinct when the instincts and attributes they are referring to have nothing to do with religion. When we long for peace and good will among people, these are not religious or soulful acts. When we dream of human beings everywhere living in harmony and mutual respect this is not the craving of a contrived soul but of the human organism itself. When one does something good for someone else without any external benefit, the resulting good or warm feeling we enjoy has nothing to do with religion. We hold ourselves out to others of our own kind and we feel lovingly toward them. This has nothing to do with religion. These emotions, drives, and needs are part of the complex organization of our bodies that help us get through daily life in a constructive manner so that we cooperate with and assist each other rather than engage in mutual annihilation. Religious belief ensures that we see and understand ourselves in an artificial and distorted way. The inability to see ourselves as we really and naturally are is the tragic gift of religious belief.

FEAR

Fear is one of humanity's most important natural tools. In conjunction with other human tools it keeps us alive. When we see or feel danger it is because our fear mechanisms are working as they should. When we see an animal larger, stronger, and faster than ourselves we know to keep our distance. When we see landslides we keep as far away as practical. When we see flooding we get to higher ground. And when we see a fellow human angry with clenched fists, we keep our distance. Fear is a healthy thing and helps us navigate the dangers of life.

In a less obvious way fear also fosters our all-around development. Through the accumulation of experiences and events that invoke some level of fear we learn, we become confident, and we achieve wisdom. We learn about the various obstacles and dangers that present themselves through the course of daily living. We thereby become better able to deal with them and similar events in the future. We gain an overall advantage with regard to the world around us. Through time and maturity we know we can negotiate many of the obstacles and challenges we are sure to face. In conjunction with our total mental selves, these experiences become a part of our memory bank and are accessible when needed. All this makes us smarter and more competent in dealing with our world and life itself. They make us wise in that our fears from the past still guide us but without the original alarm and hesitancy. The challenges of yesterday become the reservoir of knowledge and capableness for today. Fear allows us not only to survive but to become cautious and intelligent. Navigating our way through life is no longer an ordeal but more often a challenge.

Unfortunately, early on in our development as a species, some calculating and intelligent members of communities understood that they could create artificial supernatural forces or gods and convince the less ambitious members of the group that natural events and catastrophes were caused by these supernatural forces or gods because of our inadequacies. The fear of the wrath of god was officially implanted. By explaining that these events were warnings or punishments for our human transgressions and that only they, the more calculating members, knew how to placate the gods their positions of influence and power were assured. The fear that one would not enjoy the eternal heavens unless the admonishments of the slick were followed was yet another and later use of fear. Religious belief would become a double-edged sword of fear. The first fear was the fear of god's menacing nature and the physical catastrophes that he would lay on us because of our human transgressions. The second level of fear was of eternal damnation for not following scripture. Both the transgression and the punishment were invented by religious man. The fear of eternal damnation is particularly tragic because it is so vacuous. The existence of natural disasters is real, even if the religious explanation for them isn't. But the fear of eternal damnation is contrived from the beginning. Religion, once again, expropriates our natural and healthy fears for its own purposes. The natural and good fear that made us cautious and smart was fraudulently converted to an unwholesome fear that tended to make us unthinking and dull. Religious fear is not based on fact, experience, or reason. It is based on the threatened deprivation of supernatural worlds, with their concomitant gods and heavens that have no basis in our human experience as earthly creatures. Real thought is antagonistic toward such dogmatic beliefs. Real thinking will never lead to an afterlife or eternal hell. Only blind belief supported by promises and threats can get us there.

As we know, once this fear is implanted into the mind at childhood it remains in the mind almost as a permanent fixture. We live our whole lives under this dark cloud of fear. It obscures and distorts our view of actual life. We see and experience life from the perspective of a paranoid being acted upon and always being observed and judged. Earthly life becomes a frightful test. The only way to pass the test is to meticulously follow the rules and directions set out for us in religious scripture. We follow these rules only after we are told what they say and mean. We do not develop our own interpretation of said rules because that is not how dogma works. Explanation and justification of rules would lead to thinking, and that can never be permitted. Studying scripture is not thinking; it is obedience and memorization. Obeying others all one's life leads to a profound dependence and a sad stunting of mental maturation. We lose the ability to rely on our own thinking and decision-making. Perennial dependence through adulthood is not growth and development. It is their antithesis. This type of dependence is only comfortable in a static mind. It is only when good and natural fear is misappropriated by religious dogma that fear becomes a tool of control and therein becomes an integral aspect of religious faith. This cleared the path for the perpetration of the greatest fraud on our species imaginable. For much of our history we have walked through life handicapped and in denial. This concocted fear is an important component of the grip that religious belief has on its victims.

This fear, substantively, has in itself become a major factor in the embarrassingly long endurance of religious belief. Because of our limited abilities to understand and think beyond ourselves, it is very difficult for people to get beyond what is implanted in them at an early age. The introduction of fear makes getting beyond religious dogma even more difficult, especially since fear is suppose to stay with us for our own survival and well-being. Once religious belief is implanted and the resulting fear of gods and the supernatural are inculcated in us, even the most hardworking and enlightened person can have a lifelong difficulty in getting beyond and above religiously created fear. Even in the face of an intellectual realization of the invented nature of religious belief, ridding oneself of it totally takes courage and resolve. Fear is an idea or emotion that having once found a home in us must always be dealt with. Fear when developed for natural and positive purposes must be retrievable or its use is very limited. This retrievability is still the case if fear is unnaturally and negatively based through religious dogma. Unfortunately this makes dogma more resistant to change or maturity in the human being. Even though a person may be a scientist and highly rational when engaging in scientific work he may well remain that programmed youth when it comes to religious and other supernatural areas. This well-engrained religious fear is a part of us, and intellectual maturity, being only one aspect of who we are, does not readily and fully supplant the emotional power of religious fear. The emotional response of fear is just as powerful as acquired intellect or knowledge. It is an easier path to simply convince yourself and others that you consciously retain a religious inclination in spite of all else. It is socially as though you have little or nothing to lose by going this route. Fear—once good and natural—is expropriated by religious belief and becomes a powerful tool to manipulate and control.

TO RECAPITULATE

We determined earlier that to better understand this matter of religion and god it was imperative that words be used carefully and with a clear understanding of their meaning. To that end we began by defining some crucial terms. We noted that the word *theism* means to have a belief in god or gods. Importantly we noted that this belief did not have to be associated with religious belief. A theist can well believe in god, a secular god, without having any religious belief whatsoever. Of course, many theists do believe in god as a part of their religious faith. The word *atheism* simply means that there is an absence of belief in god or gods. This does not require a disbelief in god. Most atheists are persons who simply do not have that necessary affirmative belief to qualify them as theists. Some atheists do disbelieve in god but it is not the disbelief that qualifies them as atheists—it is their lack of positive belief. Lastly, we noted that all those persons who are equivocal about god are necessarily atheists. Equivocation or uncertainty is not belief. Agnosticism therefore falls under the umbrella of atheism and is not its own third category.

These word meanings set the foundation for an important premise of these essays: that there is no legitimate or necessary connection between god and religion. Any connection between god and religion is an artificial one contrived by humans. There would be no reason at all to attach the possibility of god to that of childish make-believe in the absence of some very real human purpose or motive. Virtually all human beings go through life without ever experiencing a supernatural event or happening. In spite of this, the entire institution of religious belief is built upon the blind trust that one person has in another person's unsupported contention that there is a god and he speaks to us. This is only possible because of the early programming at youth.

The reality is that almost all human beings go through life painfully aware that in each day, like all other days, earthly affairs abide by the never changing earthly rules and parameters. For a human being the utter consistency and dependability of this state can be overwhelming. However, this never-changing reality is ours and we must accept it and embrace it as nature's beings. To give humans the power to think and to understand is absolutely contradictory to the presence of the superstition and the make-believe of religious belief. For a real god to preside over the evolution of all of life so that its highest form, humanity, would become forever small and petty is not fathomable. It is only religion and its many architects that are in need of religion's manufactured god. It seems clear that if there is an actual god, we as humans are not to be made cognizant of it. This only gives more reason to confidently navigate through this life armed with tools provided to us. We have, as humans, all the capabilities to survive and flourish in the forum provided us. This is because we are but an aspect of that very forum. The forum is us and we are the forum. The constituent particles for you and I are the constituent particles for the universe. Engaging in make-believe is an insult to our maker, if we have one.

The creation of supernatural worlds and their debilitating concerns through make-believe is a self-imposed punishment and sentence. Religion is a human concoction with horrendous individual and social consequences. Religious belief calls for faith in everything but humans themselves. In our interaction with others, religious belief fosters distrust and suspicion and hate. Dogmatists can make few accommodations to the thought and sensibilities of others. Instead of a natural morality, religious belief imposes a demeaning penal code on its followers and calls it morality. Perhaps what really separates us from other animals is our capacity for individual change and growth. To grow beyond ourselves, to see beyond custom and tradition, is a gift of the first order. It is a gift whose non-use is essential for the further continuation of religion. Religious belief tells us that life itself is not its own reward. It tells us that there is something bigger and better than earthly existence. In putting down earthly life, religious belief puts down humanity itself, for humanity is the earth and the stars and they are it. Religious dogma is not only make-believe but fraudulent. It appropriates what was natural to humanity to begin with and repackages it as its own. Because of human intellectual curiosity it is natural for us to ponder those things that might be beyond our power to grasp. Throughout time we have wondered: Where truly are we, how did we get here, and why are we here? There is hardly an end to what we do not know. Then religious belief swoops in, proffering all the answers to these great questions. Those who have religious belief claim to know all about god and his likes and dislikes. They know what god wants and expects from us. And of course they know about worlds beyond the one we actually live in.

This fraudulent enterprise expropriates the entire possibility of god for its own human purposes. Those with religious belief remake our earth and the universe itself so that they can set their eyes on other humans. They appropriate what is natural in humanity and hold it out as supernatural gifts from religious god. They claim our mental processes, both intellectual and emotional, to be eternal detachable soul and only on short-term loan to our bodies. Our bodies do not get any credit for the production and maintenance of these mental processes during life. At death, the body's mental processes simply get up and leave the body so that they can live forever at the side of god himself.

We know that morality is essential to society's creation and maintenance. Without morality there can be no society. Morality is naturally produced by collective man. However, religious belief swoops in again and turns the tables on reason by asserting that religion is essential for morality. Besides appropriating morality it yanks from our own natural selves inherent fear, love, kindness, sympathy, and other very human qualities that are integral to human survival and treats them as its own. This is what religious belief bequeaths to humanity. It gives us a tortured, distorted and contorted world.

Chapter Three

Wealth

Inordinate wealth distributed among the few is most commonly criticized as being unfair. It would seem that at a minimum fairness would dictate that the financial condition of the many be sufficient to support and sustain an adequate life. Although this is certainly true, inordinate wealth among the few has an even more deleterious effect: corrosion of authentic representative government. Inordinate wealth in the few undermines and makes illusory democratic processes and the consequent political power in the majority. In addition, great wealth in the few is also in conflict with an efficiently working capitalism, a fairer and more accessible capitalism, a capitalism that works with the interests of all participants in mind. When government is controlled by the wealthy, certain capitalistic models will result that favor the wealthy at the expense of the many. On the other hand if government is honestly working for all citizens, the capitalistic models that result are equally favorable to small business and workers generally. This is the point of real democracy: to have real political power in the hands of the many, to ensure the economic and social well-being of the many. History has taught us clearly that if political power is in the hands of the few the interests of the few will be pursued. It is for this reason that the dogmatic footings for the justification of extreme wealth in the few must be identified and examined.

As human beings, we all share a common ancestry. Because of this, each individual human is forever a part of every other human, and this connection transcends more than just a historical or chronological relationship. It provides an instinctive and illuminating feeling among us and makes collective action possible. This might have been what Adam Smith was referring to when he talked about the moral sentiment that each of us possesses. Kant may have had this in mind when he wrote about the categorical imperative and its moral basis. It may be related to Heidegger's "I-they" notion that reveals our absolute togetherness as organisms. But our instincts toward collective benefit can only be successful if our society is organized such that decisions affecting everyone are made by the many for the benefit of the many, through rational institutions that reflect who we are and that work for everyone.

The inordinate distribution of wealth among the few corrodes our ability to establish rational institutions that work for the common good. So how do the wealthy few convince the many to abandon those rational institutions? The answer is dogma. Religious dogma teaches us that earthly life is inferior to the supernatural life that awaits us. It instructs us that we can endure and overcome earthly life as long as we follow religious scripture and directives. *Secular dogma* tells us that a society based on wealth for the few is the natural order. It tells us that there is only so much wealth to go around and we should be content with what we have. It tells us that if we do not follow the political and economic policies of the wealthy few things could get a lot worse. It tells us that the natural state of affairs is for one group of us to exploit or even obliterate another group of us. This is a rejection of the natural state of unity among us based on our common humanity. To accept it is to believe in the grandest of perverted dogmas, that for a species to maim and devour itself, through institutionalized ignorance, poverty, and violence, is natural and unavoidable.

It will take more than love, good will, and sporadic good deeds for our species to endure and successfully evolve. It will take a citizenship, a moral sentiment, nurtured by rational and pragmatic ideas that include first and foremost the interests of the general public. Rather than continually regurgitating the economic dogmas of the past, every proposed idea or policy should be critically examined and then tested by reason, logic, fact, or experience. And blind acceptance of the prevailing views of the past will not prove sufficient for the future. Future thought must always include an acknowledgment that each human, by its very being, has a claim of right to function fully as a human and that this, and only this, forms the real justification for all of civil society. If the political and economic institutions of society are such that they interfere with and unduly limit the natural growth and development of the individual human being, and if they further deprive the individual of an opportunity to gain the wealth and freedom that are necessary for a good life, then society's institutions are infirm and not worthy of support.

Dogma is the tool of manipulation by which the general public is lead to think that the world is functioning properly when it actually is not. Dogmas are created and protected by the few, the wealthy, the powerful in order to garner acceptance by the masses of the injustices and inequities of the world. Dogma works because it is easier for one to accept pre-packaged dogma than to grapple with the actual, thorny problems of one's community and world. To avoid falling into the trap of dogma, we must therefore collectively and continually re-examine our ideas and assertions. Our ideas must more resemble processes than end products or ultimate conclusions. They must continually change with our changing needs and challenges. We cannot continue to accept that what we receive from those who came before is the ultimate truth or an acceptable tradition.

This is particularly important for economic ideas. We have inherited several tenets of economic dogma that should be questioned. First is the idea that there is only so much wealth to go around and that, under any other system than the status quo, the average person would have even less. We must stop thinking of economic theory as though it was one final and static thing, frozen in concrete or time or something akin to scripture. Economic theory is an imperfect tool even when used properly; it should never be used as a permanent and unassailable justification for the evils or deficiencies of the day. Capitalist countries, for example, tend to rely on the economic theories of Adam Smith. However, all Adam Smith was trying to do was to explain to some extent how the economic world of his time functioned and how it could better function. He did not intend his theories to be treated as scripture. Theories first and foremost should always be tools.

Economic theory is not neutral or objective but rather is influenced by politics, and vice versa. Economic views should always take into account the social and human effects that economic policies will have on society. But we should question what is passed off as economic science if it is used as a justification for our inability to remove or at least reduce the poverty and ignorance in our world. In such a marriage of political and economic views, dogma successfully masks the self-interests of its proponents. Instead of explanation we get justification. Instead of real concern for each and every person, we get illusions of such concern. Both political and economic debate become permanently circular and meaningless.

A second tenet of economic dogma is that personal accomplishments are solely the product of individual talent and effort. This tenet states that the current economic arrangements are not responsible for discrepancies in wealth because such discrepancies result only from differences in talent and effort. The truth is, however, that personal accomplishments are heavily dependent on historical circumstances and previously reached societal advancement. What a person or group does or can do at any point in time has a great deal to do with what others before have accomplished. For this reason no one's accomplishments can ever be said to be all his or hers. Individual effort, ingenuity, and genius are important factors as well. But the nature or level of any personal accomplishment can only be as great or as advanced as the totality of preceding human accomplishments permits. Although individual effort and endeavor is truly unique and on a personal level has to do with no one else but the doer, the accomplishment itself is still in large part the result of our species' cumulative and collective past efforts. One person on his or her own can only see or reach so far. That is why personal achievements become long-term societal or collective possessions, even though the individual doer remains the immediate and deserved beneficiary, as in the case of copyright laws. We acknowledge that personal achievements are the products of individuals living in a broader society and their achievements should thus rebound to the common good. Of course, the common good cannot be achieved if the particular and unique interests and concerns of individual members of society are disregarded or unthinkingly diminished. The common good and the respect for individual members of society must be served simultaneously. This is so because the individual human occupies two roles at the same time, one as individual member of society and the other as an aspect or component of the societal collective. Each of us experiences this duality throughout our lives: There is the self that has no meaning outside the context of other human beings and the external world itself, and there is the self that functions as a unique singularity. If the self fails to function as a unique being it will lose its own identity and value. The general good and the individual member of society are not in opposition; rather they are partners. We achieve the balance between the individual and the common good through the mechanism of political democracy. No other political process is built to accommodate this duality in a meaningful way.

The wealthy and powerful few concern themselves with their own interests alone. The general good is not a part of their reality. Wealth is a gift of society to itself and its distribution must be rational and fundamentally fair. In the larger scope all the people of the earth can properly claim to have a role in this phenomenon of step-by-step growth and should therefore derive appropriate benefit there from. No society or group can claim the accomplishments of custom, culture, science, technology, or social institutions as their own. All our human accomplishments result from the benefits of ten thousand years of civilization and the riches of the earth itself. It is because of this that the masses can justifiably reject the false and romantic dogma of completely independent individualism and can lay claim to some appropriately determined interest in the material benefit or wealth resulting from personal achievement.

Other species appear to have an instinctive need to cooperate with their own kind. Their survival frequently depends on it. But in a complex world, human beings do not have the luxury to simply act upon instinct. We must at times make conscious decisions about what we might or might not do. Because we cannot rely on a species-wide instinct for decision-making, our decisions result from the varied motives and circumstances of individuals and are as varied as those motives and circumstances. They can be good or bad, helpful or hurtful, or desirable and undesirable. Fortunately, conscious decision-making can incorporate an appreciation for others, an affinity for others, and the recognition that we need each other. We can make decisions that overcome narrow or short-term concerns with an eye to broader and long-term objectives. We can understand the need to cooperate with and benefit from each other.

This type of reasoning—which takes into account the need for cooperation, looks at long-term goals, and understands the common good—contains our ethical or moral capacity. It works cooperatively with human instinct, as our instinct alone is insufficient in such complicated environments. However, dogma interferes with this moral reasoning process. It threatens instinct and reasoning by artificially limiting choices and providing simplistic cookie-cutter answers that fly in the face of mature and reasoned deliberations. Dogma overrides instinct and prevents real thinking. When groups of people push for their own dogmatic solutions, real cooperation becomes unattainable and decision-making becomes nothing but an assertion of wills. This is why the development and continued utilization of this moral-ethical faculty is so important to real thought. With this capacity to make rational ethical decisions and to act prudently, we as a citizenry can make demands upon each other and can thereby have a degree of confidence that others will find reason to act accordingly. A rational society cannot be primarily about benefiting the few; a rational society by its very nature must benefit all. All members of society exist as ends in themselves and not simply the means for the accumulation of inordinate wealth by a few. Everyone must have the opportunity for self-fulfillment. This does not imply a utopian or strictly egalitarian society with no wealth differentials. But individual opportunity for all is an important test that any political-economic system must pass if it is to be legitimate.

How do we judge the legitimacy of a political-economic system? Human judgments are subjective; that is, we work from some original reference point. In critiquing the value and worthiness of any particular society, the appropriate reference point is the basic and undeniable reality of the human being. First, each human organism functions in an identical manner as all other human beings. Second, each of us exists as an end in itself and not as a means for someone else. Therefore and third, the interests of all members of our species must be paramount and not just the interests of the few. However, throughout almost all of the history of civil society, the social reality has provided the few with much and the many with little. Great wealth, when justified, ought to come conditionally. Individual expectations or personal greed must give way to societal needs. Wealth is the grand product of society and must never be allowed to thwart the legitimate interests of all its members. There is a reason why Adam Smith entitled his great work the *Wealth of Nations* and not the *Wealth of the Few*. Unjust economic systems and institutions should not be superimposed on society by the smartest and slickest members of that society through the constant use of dogmatic diatribe. Nor must such systems be simply the product of historical accident and apathy. We must always be able to actually modify and regulate our world. Unjust systems cannot be permitted to remain unfair and unchanged simply because tradition and dogma say so.

WEALTH DISPARITY

The last ten thousand years of human history have been a history of misery and helplessness for all but a few. Those at the top are being cared for, directly and indirectly, by those below as though this state of affairs were dictated by nature itself. But this state is not natural; if it were, there would be no need to use manipulation and ideology to maintain it. One society after another has been structured by custom and dogma so as to insure this outcome of great disparity between the many and the few. This disparity is always dogmatically justified as inevitable, necessary, or natural. Given the state or condition of the majority of human beings presently inhabiting the planet, the contemporary world has not fared much better than the ones before. Our world, like any society that functions well for the few and not so well for the many, is at its foundation a brutal society. A brutal society is not an accident or the product of human nature. It is set in place by the establishment of biased and tilted institutions held up and maintained through dogma and custom, which convince the many that things are the way they should be and that what they lack is due to their own natures. They are programmed to understand that the basic conditions in their world should not and cannot be changed without the floor beneath them opening up. This state of affairs is a malignancy afflicting the many and depriving them of a life that nature is otherwise prepared to offer. A truly enlightened and modern society cannot institutionalize a preference for one class of people at the expense of the rest. Every person must be seen as an end unto herself or himself.

The dogma that justifies the enduring nature of great wealth disparity in the United States takes several forms. The first form is the supposed dictate of economic theory that working people are rightly entitled to only that which trickles down to them. Trickle-down economics is deemed by its proponents an obvious and crucial aspect of our free enterprise system, without which the economy would malfunction and perhaps self-destruct to everyone's greater disadvantage. A second form of justification is that the average American is better off than his or her counterparts elsewhere, particularly in the third world. Since you have it better than them, do not complain. A third form is that in America everyone has a chance to really make it big—to hit the jackpot. So when one person in a million is victorious, our system is vindicated. This psychological safety valve is given further credence and vitality by the notion of survival of the fittest.

The first form of justification for the enormous disparity in material well-being among Americans is that the modest income of the working person and the burgeoning wealth of the wealthy is mandated by sound economic policy. The basis for sound economic policy according to this view is the ideology, professed over and over again, that if you take care of the wealthy, or more properly if you acquiesce in the wealthy taking care of themselves, the economy will function fine and everyone will eventually reap some benefit. Taking care of the wealthy means doing everything possible to ensure that they receive every possible ounce of profit possible from their businesses and investments. Increasing and protecting the profit of the wealthy has become the magical dogmatic formula of conservative America. For example supply-siders argue that overall well-being is best achieved by reducing taxes for the wealthiest and that this will increase investment, productivity, and income generally. Legislative policy, therefore, should always be looking to assist the wealthy. Of course, tax policy is only one of many ways by which the wealthy seek assistance and sacrifice from the many. Inherent in this economic doctrine is that if the nonvital working person remains patient, some gain will eventually trickle down to him.

Trickle-down dogma is a convenient metaphor that oversimplifies and misleads. It disguises its dogmatic trickery in a cloak of relevant-sounding economic language. It makes great wealth disparity a social-economic imperative. It treats the selfish motives of the inordinately wealthy as irrelevant to the natural workings of economic science. With a vague admission that trickle-down dogma places the wealthy in a favored position at the expense of workers, it is claimed that motive on the part of the wealthy is not relevant and that any inequities that might result by way of greater economic disparity between the few and the many is simply the best we can do. It purports that in a free enterprise system capital is virtually all that matters. It follows that if capitalism is everything, then those with capital are everything. If you have capital, government should do everything in its power to help you increase it. This is why classical economists of the nineteenth century began referring to their economic doctrine as capitalism. The term *capitalism* thereby designates a distorted and unbalanced model of a free market theory. It is a predatory capitalism that focuses only on growing capital and making the wealthy become even wealthier and that places no importance on the fortunes of workers without capital. The wealthy are viewed as the only really essential element in the economic process. They deserve all the attention and credit. The worker, the consumer, and the hard-working small business owner are invisible or are collateral damage. Rather than being treated as the essential element in real wealth creation that they are, working people are looked upon as insignificant players and largely gratuitous beneficiaries. The individual member of society, the essential component upon whom and for whom civil society is instituted, is considered to be insignificant to democratic society and as merely an economic means to an end by the inordinately wealthy. In this way trickle-down justifies the view that what actually trickles down to the working person is that which rightly should constitute his share of the pie, however small a sliver it may be. This is so even though the business owner or investor cannot make a dime without the worker's skill and labor. Trickle-down dogma justifies the reality of great wealth disparity and great wealth disparity makes dogma real. Dogma and its reality become one. When this fusion becomes embedded in the mind it is terribly difficult to get beyond because it is essentially attempting to get beyond oneself. Under current popular dogma entrepreneurs are referred to as job creators. That designation confers upon them their special place in the world of trickle-down economics. It makes the rest of us reliant upon them for life and sustenance. If you are beholden to others, you are not important or worthy. They become the doers, and the rest of us are dispensable and should be grateful for the largesse of the job creators. The contributions of the employee wealth creator are dismissed or reduced to tokenism. And yet under no genuine economic theory can the employee wealth creator's contributions ever be eliminated or replaced. The intrinsic value in labor and each person's right to the property therein was acknowledged long ago by Locke. Without them there is no wealth and no wealthy individuals.

The same universal nonreplaceability cannot be said of private entrepreneurial contributions. No economy can function without those who actually do the work, but an economy can function without private capital or ownership. In actuality private ownership is a choice that society makes or acquiesces in. Private property may well prove to be the desirable course far into the future, but it cannot function without labor. When capitalistic theory is being dogmatically applied so as to diminish the essential importance of workers, that application is suspect and pregnant with self-interest and bias. In a properly understood capitalism both owner and employee are viewed as important elements in overall societal wealth creation. It is of course more beneficial for the wealthy to argue for belief in trickle-down dogma than it is to approach the economic needs of all people pragmatically and fairly.

A second form of dogmatic justification for great disparity in wealth is that working persons in our society are faring better than their counterparts elsewhere in the world. This relativistic justification only goes to the comparative situation between American workers and other workers around the globe. It does not go to the actual needs of a worker and her or his family. When you consider the pitiful wages third-world workers earn and when you consider the poverty that is endured by those with and without employment throughout the world, the threat for American workers of joining their ranks is a powerful one. This constitutes a terrible pressure on a parent provider's psyche. It is also misleading because it assumes that we are doing better solely because of our superior economic system. Americans remain undecided whether our relative economic success is due to American greatness generally or to the system of unfettered capitalism we so frequently tout.

Attributing our economic success solely to unfettered capitalism requires a denial of our own history. It fails to take into account historical domestic realities such as continental expansion, slavery, and other forms of exploitation or the international policies based on geopolitical realities and military strength. Continental expansion permitted great numbers of Americans to go west, find a new start, and enjoy opportunities that simply were not available in more established areas. It also gave the nation access to an almost unprecedented swath of fertile farmland, albeit at the expense of Native Americans. Slavery, of course, provided centuries of free labor and the development of industry that contributed substantially to the growth and wealth of the United States. Other forms of human exploitation such as segregation, ruthless child labor practices, and race and gender discrimination all took their turns in growing the American economy. The economic "advantages" that these practices brought to the country as a whole had nothing to do with capitalistic theory.

The dogma of unfettered capitalism also ignores the international political and military realities of our national past. In the eighteenth and nineteenth centuries American economic growth was nurtured by the protectionist effect of two oceans. Since then, the US has sought and gained political and economic advantages by exploiting peoples with less economic and military power along with their natural resources. We have fought wars to open or preserve markets and to exploit peoples, their oil and minerals, and other raw materials. These policies have provided an advantage to American industries at the same time they have subjected those third-world countries to the effects of colonialism and imperialism, degrading their own living standards and economic opportunities. The more developed nations of the West extended their reach across the entire planet in order to exploit the economic weaknesses of others. At the social level these people have had their indigenous cultures, traditions, and values upended—and sometimes obliterated. At the material level the modest but sustainable economies of third-world societies were converted from economies designed to provide for the needs of community to economies designed to provide cash crops or other raw materials to foreigners. The workers in these previously self-sufficient societies had to learn to survive in this new, unnatural, and unfamiliar world. The choice was between sufficient adaptation or resistance and extinction. Once again we see that the superiority of American economic growth is due less to the inherent virtues of capitalism than the pitiful effects of Western imperialism, which has so degraded conditions in much of the rest of the world.

In the end, comparisons with third-world economies are irrelevant. One cannot justify inequality or injustice by saying that inequality or injustice is worse elsewhere. What matters is whether a person has sufficient material wealth and psychological peace to gain an acceptable life in whatever society they live in. It should not be how much better off one is in comparison to someone else who has little or nothing.

Lastly, a third form of justification for extreme wealth disparity is the idea that it benefits everyone because anyone can become one of the wealthy few. The US is touted as the land of opportunity, a promise that great wealth is within the reach of all—and a message that failure to thrive economically is the fault of the individual, not the system. This is not so much a justification for wealth disparity as it is a means for convincing people to psychologically accept wealth disparity. This message is conveyed in the almost limitless number of dogmatic verbal expressions that pummel us every day. These verbal expressions encourage us to blame ourselves for our failures no matter how predictable those failures were from the very beginning. Looked at more closely, the stories of great financial success are elusive and have the nature of a lottery, in which many try and very few are rewarded. But the great patriotic story of America is that we control our fortunes, and if we fail to succeed, eventually our children will succeed where we did not. The implication is that our children will have better support or backup than we had which again is placing some of the blame on our own parents. This eases the weight of failure.

Blame and responsibility are key concepts in the ideology of wealth disparity. We are told that to blame the system is to blame our country, to be unpatriotic. But, even more insidiously, to blame our country is to blame our programmed and dogmatic selves; it involves turning a critical eye to our inner selves that, on a subconscious level, have participated in the ideology and have accepted those messages—messages like "anyone with hard work can become a millionaire"; "in America the sky is the limit"; and "you can become anything you set your mind to." All of these accepted expressions encourage acquiescence in the great wealth disparity that exists in America. They permit society's losers to accept their loser status and not to question why being free does not work better for them. We have been taught the dogma that in America poverty is a temporary and personal affliction that hard work can overcome. We have accepted the dogma that poverty and desperation are individual problems that cannot be blamed on society or economic systems. In a society where there are so few winners and so many losers there has to be a deep psychological basis for the acceptance of so much defeat and failure in a world that is suppose to be free and full of opportunity. The unique challenge in free societies is for it members to really be free. How we describe or categorize a society is one thing, to remove its masks and reveal its reality, is another. These expressions reveal part of the psychological conditioning that works to blur social reality and thereby justify great wealth disparity. These mental states are in different degrees entrenched in the hearts and minds of many Americans and compel them to dogmatically accept the naturalness and the inevitableness of great wealth disparity.

A form of dogma that is related to the message of economic self-determination is the classic idea of survival of the fittest. Unlike some of the other expressions we discussed earlier, this dogmatic expression can legitimately claim some footing in the very makeup of the human organism. The expression *survival of the fittest* was first coined by Herbert Spencer in the nineteenth century in the context of evolution and dissolution. However, it has been suggested that this expression emerged more from Spencer's laissez-faire economic biases and his acceptance of the Malthusian theory regarding population growth than from his general theories regarding evolution and dissolution.

Popularly, survival of the fittest is commonly understood to be an aspect of social Darwinism. During the nineteenth century, the notion of evolution was relatively new, and referring to survival of the fittest was a demonstration of one's modernism and enlightenment. However, its extension to the realm of morality was illogical and inappropriate. Greed or competing viciously without regard to others may be common, but it is not the result of evolution or natural selection. Darwin's theory of natural selection had to do with organisms possessing certain characteristics that, because they turned out to be favorable to their environment, gave those organisms an advantage in survival. This natural and unintended process is a far cry from what people think of when they think of survival of the fittest in the realm of morality, a notion used to justify willful or intended acts of people as they deal with others.

It is important to distinguish here between the survival instinct and the notion of survival of the fittest. Our individual drive to survive has to do with an individual exerting sometimes mundane and at other times dramatic efforts to protect oneself or to continue to exist and to stay alive. This has little to do with prevailing over others. There could be situations where the survival instinct and the need to prevail over others operate in a parallel fashion, but that would be coincidental and does not mean that the two concepts are synonymous. The survival instinct may lead a person to choose his own self-interest over that of others, but survival of the fittest, on the other hand, has more to do with competing with others for advantage no matter what the cost. Therefore, self-interest and the general survival instinct should not be confused with the idea of survival of the fittest. Self-interest may be the engine that makes capitalism go, but it is not the ethic or biological impulse to prevail over others at all costs.

With regard to fundamental human drives, it might be argued, although incorrectly, that Nietzsche's "will to power" provides a basis for the notion of survival of the fittest. Nietzsche held that the dominant force within any organism, human or nonhuman, is a will to power—a need to prevail over all pertinent forces in one's world, internal as well as external, in order to get beyond our present self and to become something more. The will to power may provide the life energy that enables us to prevail over circumstances and conditions, but it does not absolutely require the exploitation of others. It is just as compatible with that which allows a Picasso to do what he did as it is for a Bonaparte to do what he did. Both individuals demonstrated a drive to expand their capabilities and accomplishments, but only one of them sacrificed the lives and well-being of others in order to achieve that.

It is clear, after considering natural selection, the general survival drive, and the will to power, that survival of the fittest has no more of a fundamental basis than do any of the other expressions we have discussed above. The human organism has, on the one hand, a multiplicity of needs and drives and, on the other, basic intellectual and emotional limitations. Because of this, each of us is susceptible to all manner of conditioning. These verbal expressions of economic dogma do not reflect society's conscious, thought-out choices but rather our susceptibility to tradition and dogma in which reason has little influence. That these choices have been made for us does not make them right or constructive or fair or good. Great and growing wealth disparity as an accepted condition in our free society is clearly a product of dogmatic custom and tradition. As discussed by Rawls, no one considering to begin a new society would do so if there was going to be great wealth disparity and he was not one of the lucky few. You would not agree to it if you were to be one of the poor or one of the inadequately paid workers. You would not agree to it if your children were to be assigned pitiful and unfulfilling existences. Unfortunately, because of our limited natures as human beings, through custom and dogma, the few through their power-based devices can inflict damage, large and small, upon the many, and the many, sadly and all too often, cannot discern or appreciate the trickery that victimizes them.

WEALTH, POWER, AND DEMOCRACY

Coexistence between a meaningful democracy and a fair capitalistic model cannot effectively occur unless government, at all levels, is protected from the undue influence of the wealthy. The wealthy will always pursue their self-interest. They can do this best when the government gives them priority and is responsive to their needs. Their primary need, increasing their wealth, is almost always inconsistent with the interests of employees and is frequently inconsistent with the interests of the general public. A government that protects worker's rights and interests is almost always problematic to the interests of the wealth. A government that fully concerns itself with the interests of the general public is frequently problematic to the wealthy. A real democracy is a government that refuses to function in the narrow and selfish interests of the wealthy at the expense of the general public. The notion that the well-being of all individuals is best achieved through meaningful democratic processes is not an empty abstraction. True democracy will operate for the good of all, not just the wealthy few, but currently there is a great chasm between American democratic ideals and American democratic reality—a chasm that political-economic dogma seeks to obscure. It blurs the existence of that chasm between ideals and reality through dogmatic rhetoric that explains or interprets everything that is done politically to further the interests of the inordinately wealthy as being with in a sound democratic context.

The use of dogmatic rhetoric is key to undermining true democracy. Democracies are vulnerable if not fragile creatures. A government may continue to survive but the democracy that was its original nature can be undermined through the artful use of dogmatic doctrine and propaganda, leaving the mask of democracy without a truly democratic process underneath. The truth is that to the extent that the influence of the general public dwindles, so does democracy dwindle. The many do not have the luxury to be in denial. The wealthy ruling classes of the past were quite content before the advent of political liberalism and its democratic tenets. They tried their best to prevent it. For the last two or three hundred years democracy has been an irritant to the inordinately wealthy, the friend and the protector of the many and a thorn in the side of the privileged few. Because the wealthy few could not stop it, they have diluted it instead, using their inordinate wealth to propagate their relentless dogma. For example, the wealthy have used the First Amendment right to free speech to justify spending unlimited sums of money on elections and control the elected officials to act in their interests. The result is that democracy itself is trumped by the First Amendment, which was originally instituted to protect democratic processes. Such views pervert the true intentions of democracy, which includes protecting the common good. Turning again to the First Amendment, the right to free speech is protected but is not absolute. One cannot yell "fire!" in a crowded movie theatre because free speech is constrained by the need to avoid harm to others. The same might be said of unlimited monetary contributions to elected officials, which make those officials servants of the wealthy few rather than servants of the common good. However, the wealthy have obscured this reality through dogma and the familiar marketing tool of constant repetition. Repetition works in business life, and it works in political life. It precludes a discussion of competing ideas. Voters are never persuaded or convinced; they are just molded. Such is the power of unreasoned and illogical dogmatic thought. The advent of historical political liberalism may soon be a closed chapter in human history if the danger presented by the wealthy to democracy is not seen for what it is.

With great wealth comes, among other things, great power. And it is this power that is used to contaminate and manipulate government. The use of this power can make the values, principles, and goals of the majority irrelevant and meaningless. It makes government officials work for the interests of the wealthy whose interests are often inconsistent with and contrary to those of the general public. It vitiates a basic characteristic of real democracy, that every citizen have a meaningful and equal voice in government. If government is owned and controlled by the wealthy, democracy becomes merely a mask to conceal that ownership and control, and free enterprise and real democratic participation are only illusions.

The greatest evil in American political and economic life is the ingrained and relentless process whereby the wealthy (1) purchase the loyalty of elected officials through campaign contributions and (2) cash in on that loyalty through lobbying efforts for policies that benefit them financially. What is created is a veil of ostensible democracy that covers up the real ownership of our government. After ridding ourselves of emperors, kings, queens, and dictators, we in the twenty-first century find ourselves in the same situation as previous generations but with the actors in different costumes. As long as there is great wealth in the few, a protective wall must be built between it and democratic government. This wall must prevent the wealthy from using their wealth to purchase politicians and political dominance. To insulate government from manipulation by the wealthy, financing political campaigns must be a public matter, at public expense for a very public purpose. Then political dogma may become political dialogue and nonthinking will be replaced by the weighing and consideration of ideas. What is best for society will become the issue and dogmatic slogans of fear and hate will have no place. Political candidates will be better challenged and their worth better measured. Political campaigns will no longer be the forum for battle between wealthy gladiators. Eliminating the prerogatives of the wealthy to buy governments, and to thereby prevent the wealthy from stealing government away from the people, will comprise the greatest social and political challenge Americans and other would be free people will face in the future. Unfortunately protecting government from the wealthy and powerful has never really been accomplished. If eliminating the prerogatives of the wealthy were to be accomplished, the experiment in real democracy could truly begin.

CRITICAL MASS

There was a time when the European kings and queens of the world were in virtually complete control of their kingdoms. Their subjects were most often powerless and poor. Everyone knew their role in society—peasant, noble, priest—and these roles were permanent and often passed on from generation to generation. Monarchs derived their right to rule directly from god, according to the dogma of divine right. The legitimacy of the notion of divine right was challenged by Locke in his *First Treatise,* but still we find, even today, that most societies are still organized as pyramids, with a few powerful at the top and the many powerless at the bottom. The new kings and queens have been replaced by the inordinately wealthy and their giant corporations. They too have dogmas to justify their favored position in society.

The modern dogma that justifies rule by the few is the doctrine of critical mass. The dogma of critical mass states that society only functions if the rich are kept rich and that economic stability is threatened by the spread of wealth among all members of society. It is a dogmatic, unreasoned view that justifies the near universal state of the many being at the bottom and the few at the top; and it contains within it an implied threat to those who might want to up-end tradition and the status quo. It is a doctrine that we have all been programmed to believe in. The idea is that if the average guy receives too much of the pie and the rich do not keep getting more and more that a critical mass will be reached and a mysterious equilibrium will be fatefully tipped and the economy will collapse and the average person will be even worse off than before. If this is not a threat to the many I do not know what is. A king or queen of the past might have threatened eternal damnation to a subject for violating god's commandment. Today the wealthy threaten the many an even more pitiful subsistence. The common people are encouraged to be content with what they have lest, while striving to get more, they fall into further poverty. The wealthy claim that they deserve everything that they have. They contend that the economy is not really a partnership between all members of society but rather that they are responsible for all the economic prosperity a society may have. Their one-sided approach is consistent with the doctrine of classical and trickle-down economics, narrow categories of capitalism that they insist are the only true guarantors of prosperity.

This view implies that there is only one true capitalistic theory. But in truth there are many types of capitalism, and capitalism can be modeled to protect the well-being of the many as well as the few. Any model chosen should be the consequence of reason and should be fair to all—it should not just consistently favor the interests of the few. Our economic models may have changed on the surface—from feudalism to capitalism—but the core structure of favoring the few at the expense of the many has not. The embattled subjects of past kings and queens have simply evolved into the psychologically extorted poor and working classes of today. For the most part, people accept the world as it is and feel that the way things are is the way things must be. The many do not realize that things are as they are because the few have determined it so. They do not appreciate the role that human will and drive play in the makeup and character of communities and societies. Their dogmatic belief systems justify all.

It is essential to cast off ideology if we want to create a more just world. If a particular capitalistic model cannot be made to be sufficiently effective in an economic sense and sufficiently fair in a human sense, then we can apply critical thinking to the deficiencies of the system and improve it. Dogma tries to make present systems sacrosanct and untouchable. But we can get beyond dogma, get beyond our dogmatic selves, to engage in real applied thought about our public and private concerns. Change is the birthright of all future generations. Through a proper and measured use of government, as partner and protector, some balanced model can be arrived at that would achieve greater fairness and have the ability to address more of the needs of all members of society. Economic and social structures are not scripture handed down by god or past generations of Americans. Theories and any resultant social or economic structures must be treated as tools for the betterment of all and not as eternal dogma that can never be questioned.

Up to now the mechanism of a mixed economy—part free market, part government involvement—has been selected as an important and practical way to achieve societal goals, but that mixed economy has been heavily tilted toward the needs and desires of the wealthy. In fact, when government interference in the free market has taken place, it has often been for the benefit of the rich and for large corporations, creating something like a corporate welfare state. Since the inception of America the purveyors of economic dogma have traipsed the halls of government so as to reduce or eliminate their business risk, increase or insure their margin of profits, and pursue their own specific interests. Far from seeing government as a hands-off entity in economic development, the rich and business interests have always utilized the American government to manage the economy on their behalf. For the wealthy, affecting government policy and legislation is good business. They cannot profit so surely and so well without doing so. Advantage and special treatment are the tools of their trade.

The wealthy often tout the importance of laissez-faire policy, meaning the non-interference of government in the workings of the free-market economy. However, their advocacy of laissez-faire economics exists only as another deceitful illusion supported on a foundation of dogma. The dogma is that the wealthy and big businesses oppose laissez-faire; the reality is that they are the ones who constantly push for government involvement—on their own behalf. The government is encouraged to be as active as it needs to be to further the interests of the wealthy, involving itself in any legislation and policy making that will clear the way for the wealthy. The wealthy and big business are happy to accept government assistance. It is only when the general public seek from their government assistance in economic and social matters that the wealthy loudly blow the bugle of laissez-faire. It is imperative then, that future generations of Americans attempt to find a home for the application of reason, practicality, and fairness when further molding crucial governmental and economic institutions. If this does not occur, the corruptive nature of the unrestrained power of the inordinately wealthy will forever end America's grand experiment.

In the minds of most people laissez-faire stands for non-interference or non-involvement by government in economic matters of society. To the wealthy and more savvy, laissez-faire stands for something quite different. It is an important part of their dogmatic word game that allows them and them alone to hypocritically function dualistically. The rest of us remain in Plato's cave trying to deal with the illusions cast by its deceitful shadows. According to the interpretation of the wealthy, laissez-faire compels different treatment for the wealthy and the many. It implies that the government's primary client should be the wealthy. The government is encouraged to be as active and non-passive as it needs to be to further the interests of the wealthy. The government is encouraged to be as active as it needs to be so long as those efforts are directed to the advantage of the wealthy. Government should, in a non-laissez-faire way, actively involve itself in any legislation and policy making that will clear the way for the wealthy. Active government assistance is sought by the wealthy whenever employee interests must be ignored or denied. It is when the many or the general public seek from their government assistance in economic and social matters that the wealthy loudly blow the bugle of laissez-faire. In other words if any social or economic legislation or policy might somehow positively affect the interests of the many such government activity should not be engaged in because that would violate the sacred dogmatic notion of laissez-faire. The hypocritical nature of laissez-faire is covered up by its dogmatic masks. Therefore laissez-faire dogma permits governmental concern and activity when it benefits the wealthy and encourages government to close its eyes to the interests of the many. That government at times is trying to protect or further other valid societal interests is beside the point.

The hypocrisy of the wealthy regarding laissez-faire capitalism is only matched by their refusal to play by the rules of capitalism itself. With influence and power the rules of capitalism, as well as the rules of democracy, can be flouted by the wealthy. Capitalism contemplates the application of capital to some venture and undergoing certain risks and uncertainties. But traditional notions of capitalism become meaningless when the wealthy are provided with low-risk and high-yield opportunities through special treatment by the government. This favoritism is mostly extended to the large corporations. For the most part, small businesses have to live within the dictates of laissez-faire capitalism demands and therefore function within an actual capitalistic reality. They are not too big to fail. The wealthy talk about capitalism, but the small businessperson lives capitalism and talks business. We must never confuse the world of the inordinately wealthy with that of the small business owner who attempts daily to survive and prosper within the parameters of capitalistic demands. In many instances small business owners are both owners and workers. They are the builders of real societal wealth. It is important therefore in analyzing economic-political matters not to lump together the inordinately wealthy with hard-working business owners. They play different roles in our society. One is a contributor from beginning to end while the other takes and takes without giving back.

It's clear that the wealthy advocate a kind of laissez-faire dogma that is disconnected from reality and serves to obscure the way they use government to their own advantage. Capitalism as an expression becomes just a word that justifies the wealthy in doing whatever it wants whether within or without the logical parameters of capitalistic principles. Capitalism then magically becomes a justification for business running rough shod over the interests of the general public as if there was some compelling moral and economic imperative to do so. The economic philosopher known as the father of capitalism, Adam Smith, never actually advocated real laissez-faire. Smith understood that the interests of business are often harmful to and in conflict with the interests of the general public. He saw government's role as protecting the public's interest, and he cautioned against things like monopolies and preferential legislation. The title of Adam Smith's great work *The Wealth of Nations* is telling. It was to be an explanation for the wealth of *nations*, not the wealth of the *wealthy*.

A different view is that government's primary client should be the American people as a whole. The government's primary mission would be to ensure that business activity, even at the highest levels, functions ultimately as a tool that works for all of society and not at the expense of the American public. The dishonest discussion about socialism versus capitalism, or big government or small government, is misleading. We have always had government involvement in the economy. The question becomes: involvement on whose behalf? The discussion should be about when, where, and how the government should intelligently and pragmatically involve itself in specific economic matters so as to ensure the well-being of our nation as a living democracy while also nurturing a positive business environment.

TOOLS OF CONTROL: DOGMA, MONEY, AND THE CORPORATION

Of all the dangers that have threatened and do threaten American political freedom, none is as ominous as great wealth accumulation in the few. Concentration of great wealth among the few means that a small sector of society, through campaign contributions, has undue influence in legislation. They can influence the tax code, get government subsidies for their industries, and steer government spending away from educational and social opportunity for the general public and toward expenditures (like military contracts) that benefit themselves. With inordinate wealth in the few all that remains is old-fashioned oligarchy hiding behind an illusion of democracy.

How specifically do the wealthy manipulate the government to maintain their own wealth and power? They have two central weapons in their arsenal: dogma and money. Through dogma, they can convince the public—and government officials—that policies that benefit the wealthy are in the best interest of all. The holding in the 2010 United States Supreme Court case of Citizens United, which disallowed caps on campaign contributions, is one example. The dogma of the wealthy was persuasive in its assertion that buying government by the inordinately wealthy for personal and selfish reasons is a function of First Amendment free speech rights. The changing of reality, our perception of political reality, is achieved when we are convinced that the wealthy are only living out the dictates of constitutional mandates and that this is ultimately for the benefit of the many.

Manipulating the electoral process is key to ensuring control of the government for the wealthy. Real democracy can in part be judged by the openness, inclusiveness, and fairness of the electoral process. Does the electoral process truly provide a mechanism by which the sentiments of the many can be heard? Or has the electoral process been sufficiently undermined so that the voice of the wealthy is heard above all others? Having an "election" is not enough; an electoral process can be meaningful or it can be a sham. No factor, at least in America, is more important in determining the sham nature of the electoral process than money. Money leads to influence, and influence to power. Money helps determine who gets elected and who gets favors. It does not have to be like this. Effecting free elections so that they are no longer free does not have to be a perk of great wealth. In fact it should never be, and in the long run it cannot be if real democracy is to ever regain a more meaningful and enduring presence in the life of America.

The auto mechanic, the grocery clerk, you, and I know that politicians are regularly bought through direct contributions to a particular candidate's campaign. We also know that if large amounts of money are indirectly spent to assist someone's election effort that the effect is the same as a direct contribution to the actual campaign. In either case, the benefits to the large contributors are clear: special access to legislators and influence regarding legislation. It is different with small contributors. The small contributor or noncontributor who expresses his views to an elected official understands that his views will only be acted upon if an overwhelming number of other voters clearly and forcefully express similar feelings. This is as it should be, since legislation should reflect the well-being of the majority. A large contributor, however, expects his views to be acted upon by legislators regardless of whether many others hold the same view. His influence flows from his wallet and not by virtue of his view being held in common with many others. This is not true democracy, and what follows are policies that end up making societies unfair and the world hostile.

Another way in which the wealthy few control the government is through lobbying efforts. Large corporations and whole industries spend staggering amounts of money on lobbying. This would not be the case if the enormous amounts of money spent did not bear fruit. Lobbying is the mechanism by which corporations and the wealthy extract legislative favors from the elected officials to whom they contributed during the campaign stage. It serves to quell real debate and drown out any attempted meaningful exchange of ideas and interests among the many. Lobbying is also a powerful tool of dogma. In ads and public service announcement, the language that feeds the airwaves and print space is narrow, deceitful, and tactical dogma. It does not involve the exchange of real competing ideas but only involves the dishonest spread of fear and hate.

The bottom line is that great sums of money are a corrupting influence on American politics. Campaign contributions have a great influence on who gets elected and on who owns the elected official, and lobbying is the mechanism both for extracting favors and for reinforcing dogma. Ownership by corporate America of America has become the rule of the day. Ownership of the President and the Congress should be in the general public, not in the few inordinately wealthy whose only agenda is to increase their wealth and power. The only truly effective way to eradicate this cancer is to institute publicly paid campaigns. For most Americans this does not sound like a preferred course. But given the reality—the reality that our government is now truly up for sale—there is no other viable option, at least if saving democracy is priority. Unfortunately lesser measures will probably prove ineffective as great wealth has a way of getting around well-intended obstacles. The oligarchic forces will claim that it is their god-given American right, through the use of corporate clones, to compete against lesser monied humans. They believe, but will not admit, that even governments should be for sale.

The role of corporations in American politics has become particularly troublesome. By the early 1800s, the general business corporation had become a common feature in American commercial affairs. Legislation pertaining to corporations was already being enacted. Over time and up to the present the federal government and various state governments through the passing of legislation, and rendering of judicial decisions, have authorized limitations on corporations making financial contributions, directly and indirectly, to and for political candidates. The problem is that by acknowledging the government's right to control or regulate is the implied admission that corporations could in fact participate at least to some extent in the political process. Instead of passing blanket legislation forbidding political involvement by corporations or rendering judicial decisions to the same affect, the piecemeal approach has led to a situation of active corporate participation in all areas where they are not expressly forbidden, areas that are getting smaller and smaller with each passing year.

Now we find that, with little debate, we have come to accept acknowledgement of the corporation as a political entity with the same or greater rights and influence as individuals. This was clearly seen in the *Citizens United* decision that struck down any limits on campaign contributions. On the judicial side there is less myopia but more dogma. To conclude that wild corporate spending in American politics is protected by the individual right of free speech reveals an oligarchic bias that has never really been absent from American politics and that utilizes dogmatic language to mask over true intentions. These intentions are rooted in fear and mistrust of true democracy. Logic is not self-executing. It must have a sound beginning and a reasonable end. The free speech rights of human beings should not be fraudulently used to undermine American democracy. To argue that corporate America's buying of our government is protected by the constitutional right to free speech is among the ultimate perversions of logic and reason.

The corporation has evolved from being first a business tool, then a political tool, then a political weapon, and finally a leviathan ruling its creator. Corporations are legal fictions created by the legal system. They are meant to aid entrepreneurs and investors in building business ventures. It provides them with various financial, tax, and logistical advantages. But the role of the corporation has strayed from its original role of a simple business tool until now it functions as a powerful actor in politics.

This is not a natural or inevitable role. Corporations can only stray from their original role limited to business matters if the various branches of government desire it or permit it to do so. The preamble of the American Constitution reads "We the People," not "We the Corporations." The nation of the United States was created by human beings for human beings. Nowhere in the Constitution is there any room for the exercise of discretion and judgment by the corporate legal fiction. Within the polity, corporations should have no existence. They should not vote or hold office. Nor should they contribute to the political process by purchasing election victories and politicians so as to ensure control over government at the expense of the many.

So how did we get to this point? Apparently by the early eighteen hundreds the general business corporation had become a common feature in American commercial affairs. Legislation pertaining to corporations was already being enacted. Over time and up to the present the federal government and various state governments through the passing of legislation, and rendering of judicial decisions, have authorized limitations on corporations making financial contributions, directly and indirectly, to and for political candidates. The veiled problem is that by acknowledging the government's right to control or regulate is the implied admission that corporations could in fact participate at least to some extent in the political process. Instead of passing blanket legislation forbidding political involvement by corporations or rendering judicial decisions to the same affect, the piecemeal approach has led to a situation where the manmade monster is ready and able to destroy the master's castle.

As early as 1819 Chief Justice Marshall in *The Trustees of Dartmouth College v Woodward* wrote, "A corporation is an artificial being, invisible, intangible, and existing only in contemplation of law." In his dissent in *Citizens United*, Justice Stevens quotes President Theodore Roosevelt speaking to Congress in 1905: "All contributions by corporations to any political committee or for any political purpose should be forbidden." Permitting corporate political participation through financial contribution of any sort or amount is giving away America's ability to defend itself from within. Real democracy and the American way of life are being taken away from us one legislative enactment and one judicial decision at a time.

We must find a way to break away from the dogma of the corporation and return to our democratic roots. In America we are accustomed to relying on the viability of our political institutions. They are not perfect but in the long run, with some notable and profound exceptions, they seem to have served us relatively well when it comes to respecting and protecting the individual. But what do we do when our political institutions keep doing things that seem to be leading us down a primrose path? When free speech is interpreted such that it permits the inordinately wealthy through their corporations to buy our government at the expense of democracy? When the Supreme Court, which is supposed to protect democracy, permits the inordinately wealthy to own it and control it? The first step is to reject the iron grip of dogma. We can reject dogmatic justifications. We can reject dogmatic language that always protects the special interests of the wealthy at our expense. Clear and real thinking is our only truly effective tool. If utilized sufficiently, everything else will eventually, although painstakingly, take care of itself.

We cannot continue on with a blind faith in the indestructibility of American democracy. We must take our thoughts and actions back into our own hands. That a Supreme Court justice or a member of Congress or the president or anyone else says that a corporation or a wealthy individual has a "right" to spend all the money in the world for political purposes does not make it so. After all, this "right" of free speech through excessive campaign contributions or corporate spending can effectively make your view—the views of all individuals without those same financial resources—irrelevant or of no consequence. When expressing one's view on social matters becomes an empty act or becomes irrelevant, then the free speech protections have been made meaningless. When great wealth through corporate masks can insulate government officials and government itself from the words and opinions of the many, then great wealth has succeeded in making free speech irrelevant. You cannot have a democracy where government and government officials listen to money and not to the people. Given the magnitude of the problem and the enduring consequences that inevitably follow, acquiescence and acceptance are not options. Theft of real democracy from Americans by the wealthy, frequently through their corporate weaponry, must be thwarted; otherwise our posterity will truly be victims of a consummated crime. The tragedy will be that our posterity will have been dogmatically programmed to believe that they are still enjoying the fruits of a real and unique democracy.

WHY IT MATTERS

Does real democracy matter? Spinoza, many years ago, explained and justified democracy as being the form of government best suited to ensure that each person's natural self is protected and promoted. Spinoza's core idea is that each human organism functions in an identical way as all other human organisms. What each human being experiences is of the same stuff that all other humans experience. There is nothing fundamentally different or special about one person in comparison to another person. Each of us is complete within ourselves. Understanding this, it would make little sense to construct a society in which many are routinely exploited by the few, where the many experience life on a lesser scale than the few, and where the many endure while the few thrive. We are not talking about some form of distributive egalitarianism but a profound form of individual freedom that is necessary for continual development and a full life. Where everyone has a meaningful voice in political and social matters, this shared commonality will on its own promote a natural and mutual self-interest that benefits all of society's members.

Hence the importance of real democracy as that form of government best suited to ensure that each of us and all of us can truly be ourselves, our natural and complete selves. Each of us has the same interest and motivation to see that this is accomplished. This natural harmony, however, is invariably broken by the inordinately wealthy. It is through disharmony that the wealthy orchestrate their violent music. Prevailing over others is the constant theme. The addictiveness of wealth and power flourish only at the expense of others. Having fallen out of that natural harmony, the wealthy live in that constant fear that only presents itself in the jungle of war and dominance. They find it foreign and awkward to function in an atmosphere of trust and confidence. And their need for more wealth and power is never satisfied. With wealth comes power over others and the power to generate more wealth. These two insatiable drives become the driving forces in our politics, our economies, our law, and our decision making.

When the insatiable drives of power and money on the part of the wealthy few become the basis for our society, the only way to combat it is through critical thinking. We rely on tradition and dogma almost unconsciously, similarly to a bodily motor reaction. Societies continually deal with a multitude of social, economic and political matters. In more closed societies this is done, for the most part, internally and among governmental operatives. The more open a society is to dialogue, the more decision making will also include the general public in some form. If the wealthy few want to keep the status quo, they must rely on dogma to neutralize the participation of the public in decision making, and dogma is their instrument of neutralizing public participation. The general public has become all too comfortable with the language and non-thought of dogma, eschewing facts and specifics. Dogma convinces the many not only to support the interests of the wealthy but that their own important concerns are being met by the status quo.

Dogma can take on many forms. Some views or ideas are dogmatic from the start—beliefs wherein reason, experience, and fact never made an appearance. Some views were originally the product of human reason but were later mistreated and became dogmatic in appearance and application. An example of this would be the constitutionally guaranteed right to free speech. The right to free speech was an important achievement, the product of past political experience, courageous human sacrifice, and intellectual advancement. Our court system has, however, through one dogmatic application after another, turned this pillar of democracy into a destroyer of democracy. This constitutional directive has been reinterpreted in such a way that it is being used to put the final touches on an American oligarchy.

If the general public, the many, would more frequently engage in reasoned thought and less frequently on blind reliance on dogmatic slogans the general public would more perfectly follow their own self-interest and thereby the interests of society as a whole. Rational thought would lead them to the conclusion that life does not have to be so unfair, that life could be qualitatively better for everyone, that the good things they do have are not just attributable to one unique approach to economics, and that the purpose of democracy and free enterprise was to change the historical reality that the many should live for the few. The ironic thing is that those with real power and wealth are not dogmatic. They speak dogmatically for public consumption. However, they cannot afford to be dogmatic—that is to say, irrational and muddy-headed—in their business or professional activities. The rest of us need to do the same. Only through the use of critical thinking can the general public discern its own true self-interests. If the general public ever reaches the point where it can see and think clearly, the inordinately wealthy and powerful will shake in their boots.

The wealthy try to convince us, through dogma, that our only choice is between a static predatory model of capitalism and a lifeless conforming socialism. But if we can get beyond dogma and not be afraid to confront the world with reason and objectivity, many other models are possible. The end game of a predatory capitalism would be to continually increase the wealth disparity between the few and the many to its ultimate limit. The end game of a lifeless socialism is to unthinkingly make all wealth disparity disappear. This would in all likelihood result in a deadening psychological and emotional straitjacket for the many. Both options would lead to a result that is flatly inconsistent with individual freedom and growth. But economic theory need not be perfect to be useful. We can draw from each theory what is useful to create new models. More and more sophisticated economic theories might even contain, internally, noneconomic considerations that are of great value to society. We might follow the lead of science, which functions without this crude either/or attitude. In science, for example, both relativity and quantum theories have been found to be useful concurrently. Therefore, each has a role. And during all this, pursuit of a more comprehensive unified theory goes on. Why cannot the same rational approach be taken in economic, social, and political life? There is no reason why future generations should not always be attempting to develop better suited economic theories and strategies that will better serve the world's people. Economic theories and approaches must be made compatible with higher social and political realities and needs. Our responsibility through the use of greater real thinking is to make our world a better and fairer place. Our challenge will be to not continually shackle future generations with programmed dogma that ensures the status quo, injustice, and needless pain upon the many. We must approach each theory, and each proposition within that theory, with rationality and clear thinking. Theory must be tested against experience and knowledge and never simply accepted as dogma. Most important, each theory must be tested for its ultimate value: whether it helps human beings. Only then can we get beyond dogma and place it in the ash heap of history.

Chapter Four

Nation-State Lawlessness

Rule of law is the foundation for a constructive and productive community or world. A society that is neither stable nor ordered is unable to take advantage of the unique benefits of cooperative human effort. Given the right set of circumstances the human organism is by its very nature capable of, and amenable to, living and cooperating with others of its own kind. The right set of circumstances begin with law and order. Law and order provide confidence that one's safety is ensured and that one's labor and acquisitions are secure. They provide confidence that long-range planning and sacrifice will not go to waste on someone else's whim. They are the basis for all successful human efforts to live cohesively and productively.

Although we often pay tribute to the rule of law, we tend to think of it in terms of the local or national level. But the same law and order that is necessary for successful local or national societies is also necessary for international cooperation. Yet, because of dogma, we fail to apply the same standards of law and order to nation-states. When there is international conflict, we tend to blame it on our defective human nature. We may blame other peoples, individual leaders who are particularly "evil," or governments whose ideologies differ from ours. Americans also hold that much of the rest of the world is just jealous of us and for that reason pose an imminent danger to us.

But what if instead these conflicts were caused by the inherent lawlessness of the nation-state system itself? Although we try to limit lawlessness or anarchy through the pretensions of treaties and summit conferences, lawlessness does not disappear by simply signing papers and agreeing to international laws. This is because international law is not really law. A key component of true law is enforcement; unenforceable law is not law in any meaningful sense. And because ultimately there is no legitimate and actual coercive authority to enforce international law, it is an illusion. Despite the good intentions behind the creation of the United Nations, the UN is not a government with coercive authority. It is only a vehicle by which multiple nations can determine whether or not they agree on a course of action on a case-by-case basis.

Supranational organizations like the UN may have modest benefits, but ultimately they provide only illusions of meaningful and cooperative dialogue and interaction. Their efforts can in fact obscure the central fact of international relations today: that international relations take place in a state of lawlessness. Nations are exempt from any real global governance. As a global species we are presently and simply wrongly organized. Although the human organism is sufficiently flexible to be collectively constructive or destructive we are not sufficiently advanced or mature to do the right thing because it is the right thing to do. Reason dictates that it is an absolute requirement to our living together constructively that we be correctly organized, that we all live under a system of law and order. The word "system" in the nation-state context is actually a misnomer. The presence of nation-states worldwide does not constitute a system and that is, in fact, the core problem. Nation-states are not so much a result of some systematic rational design but have emerged, historically, out of the random acts of force and greed of individuals and corporate bodies. With regard to the needs and interests of varied ethnic, cultural, and geographical groups of people, nation-states have proven arbitrary and ineffective.

Because of their random provenance and their essential lawlessness, nation-states have frequently proven to be an obstacle or barrier rather than a tool or vehicle in furtherance of the interests of people throughout the world. To be a system the parts of the whole must work in tandem. Our species naturally constitutes one whole. We are all progeny from the same biological ancestral form, we all function in the same way, and we all occupy the same finite space. We are interdependent, a fact that becomes more apparent as the world becomes smaller. Our sameness does not ensure cooperation and cohesion; love, good will, and prayer do not get the job of peaceful and constructive co-existence done. What is required is that the rule of law must encompass the entire system, that our unity as a species be matched with a unity of law and order, one that is applied equally across the world. Therefore, to move beyond lawlessness we must move beyond the present obsolete and anarchistic nation-state reality.

Lawlessness cannot be solved by the nation-state because the nation-state is, by definition, a subgroup of people joined together by a common law but exempt from the law of other nation-states. Inasmuch as lawlessness is inherent in the nation-state's nonsystematic nature and since it cannot by definition be removed from the nation-state reality, the whole of our species has a dire need for singular and global self-government. At the global level, all of the world's people must live under the same enforceable rules and this is only possible if they all live under the purview and protection of the same government. At the regional or local levels flexibility in the law would be warranted and rational. Our species is quite capable of self-government on any scale, large or small. But without a government that is equally responsible to and for all the people of the world, there cannot be a sufficient system of laws that is adequate to secure for all such inhabitants the blessings of order and fairness.

Anything short of a global governance will always contain the seeds of discord and continual power based resolution of disputes. Global order requires that all the people of all the nations of the world be bound at the global level by one body of law that is mutually beneficial to all and also enforceable. After all, government at its simplest and best is that process whereby everyone buys into a mutually beneficial order secured through enforceable and universally accepted law. The avoidance of war between and among groups or regions through mandated and peaceful resolution processes would be a primary purpose of a global government. Without one singular government representing all of the world's people our species will continue to atrophy and self-mutilate.

SOVEREIGNTY

Sovereignty is the cornerstone of nation-states. There are two faces to sovereignty: one that is the real face and one that consists of dogma. As dogma, sovereignty functions as a psychological justification for what otherwise would be considered lawless actions. We are taught that sovereignty is simultaneously the declaration of and the acknowledgement of the autonomy of any given nation-state over its own affairs and the affairs of its constituent members. We are programmed to believe that, in this permanently evil world, sovereignty is the only thing that enables us to be free. We are taught that only through national independence can we ensure for ourselves liberty and prosperity. Patriotism becomes both the mask and the shield of sovereignty and national pride, and through blind patriotism we are conditioned to do what would ordinarily be unthinkable and reprehensible.

Among all nations this fear and mistrust invariably promotes a narrow short term self-interest that lays the ground work for future discord. The universal and inherent feature of lawlessness in the nation-state reality will doom our species to a continued history of tragic disparity of opportunity and needless mayhem and death.

In reality, sovereignty means that each nation as a singular unit is independent and answerable to no one. It means that the nation is not subject to the rule of law on an international scale. These Nations function as political islands, unable to provide a basis for trust and confidence among themselves because each nation has the duty to be concerned with its own interests, with the well-being of its citizens alone. As a sovereign political entity a nation-state by its own nature owes nothing to any other nation-state. There is no right or no wrong—just survival.

This system of governance is not architectonically capable of permitting long-term cooperation and progress. There can be no trust between nations since each nation acts for its own benefit alone. It necessitates and encourages constant do-or-die competition that inexorably leads to discord and strife, winners and losers. Each nation must pursue a narrow self-interest that makes no allowance for the needs of others except in a strict Machiavellian sense. Accommodation is really made only to the power, strength, and leverage possessed by others. Nations therefore are limited only by their own relative wealth and military vulnerability. If nation A determines that nation B has something of importance that it wants, and if nation A determines that it is sufficiently strong in relation to nation B, then nation A (after conjuring up dogmatically based justifications for consumption by their own citizenry) simply takes what nation B has by force or threat of force. This is one nation acting pursuant to its own interest. There is no pretense of acting pursuant to the mutual interests of both nations. The sad truth is that within the nation-state reality, accommodation to others is unnecessary and will rarely be made on the basis of enduring mutual interests.

The resulting fear and mistrust have always been exploited by governments internally, within their own borders, so as to induce their citizens to be patriotic and ready to fight and die for their country. Nation-states—at the behest of the inordinately wealthy and big business in general—conduct foreign policy so as to further their own financial interests. This can mean acquiring mineral or plant resources; accessing cheap labor, cheap products, and new markets; opening trade routes and byways; buying off local dictators; and even starting wars on behalf of its own wealthy citizens and corporations. Domestically, nation-states must use dogma to gain the support or fervor of its own citizenry for these projects, as citizens could rarely be enticed to sacrifice or die just to fill the pockets of the wealthy. Dogma is also used to convince other nations that its actions are justified, but such convincing is optional since no real law can be applied to its actions and no sanctions enforced.

CULTURE

Culture, like morality, is requisite to the formation and continued viability of any society. It encompasses all the laws, traditions, and mindsets of a particular society and acts as a mechanism of cohesion for its members. Formal or civil law alone cannot on its own keep society stable and constructive. The mores, norms and values that constitute culture are as indispensable to society as is the law. They teach us how to perceive and understand both the world around us and ourselves with in that world. By having a common culture, members of a society know what to expect from each other and can thus function in an atmosphere of trust, confidence, and predictability.

Culture is often associated with the unique preparation of food, manner of dress, and arts of a particular society, but these are to a large extent superficial aspects of culture. How we value our lives on earth, how we value each other, how we value the need for compliance with the norm, or how we value personal choice and creativity are more fundamental aspects of culture. Unfortunately, culture can also be a divisive force. To the dogmatically programmed person, the superficial cultural forms and shapes appear as basic and as important as do to the core values of culture. Superficial differences can become major points of contention between societies. We can see this, for example, in the sometimes bitter disagreements among Catholics and Protestants over doctrine, despite their shared belief in the divinity of Jesus. To those who focus on the superficial aspects of culture, small differences are felt to be critical issues that must be defended at all costs. To the unthinking dogmatist these superficial differences—whether religious, patriotic, or racial—are worth hating and dying for. The necessary trust and comfort that culture brings to a society or world civilization are not dependent upon sameness in cultural shapes and forms. But in every society the keepers of dogmatic traditions attempt to elevate cultural differences in form and shape to irreconcilable core value differences. In fact, the nation-state reality depends upon these feared differences and the resulting fear and mistrust. We have been programmed through dogma and fear to reject the possibility of worldwide human cooperation and reject any attempt at order through law in the form of a singular democratic government.

Differences in the more superficial cultural forms and shapes among the peoples of the world do not mean global societal cohesion cannot be achieved. We do not have to all be the same. We only have to reject the dogma that attaches critical importance to superficial cultural differences and to choose to act in ways that enhance the personal dignity, freedom, and responsibility of all. For those who have grown beyond dogmatic traditions these values can never be negotiated away. Universal core cultural values must embody these human needs. The essential nature of the human organism is identical for everyone everywhere. The fundamental core values are the same for all liberated and vibrant people. When we understand that peoples everywhere when truly given the choice will opt for their own personal liberty and their own sense of contentment every time, then, we can fully appreciate how people are just people.

DOMINANT GROUPS

In every nation-state there are controlling or dominant groups. No matter what the political or economic structures of any particular nation-state, there are always the few with wealth and power at the top and the many below. These dominant groups usually have an eclectic makeup and frequently consist of the pillars of society, but they are alike in this way: Their fundamental concern is their own well-being and the maintenance of their power positions. They have the know-how and tools to assert their will and they do just that. In open societies, the dominant groups maintain their power positions through the use of dogma-based propaganda. In closed societies they rely on fear, force, or violence. In either case, they pursue their own interest at the expense of the rest of society, even if pursuing those interests requires economic disparity domestically and war and violent atrocities on the international level.

Working people possess little interest in ruthlessly competing against their counterparts domestically or around the world. This is because their material needs are not in conflict with the material needs of those counterparts. They only need the essentials of life—a finite wish list that is a far cry from the insatiable wealth and power that drives the driven. As the driven all want more and more, they do inevitably run into conflict with each other. It starts by the inordinately wealthy determining that there is great gain to be had through gaining access to, control over, or acquisition of markets, facilities, land, and the human resources found in other nations. Because they own and control government, a dominant group will use government to act on their behalf. The range of options can extend from relatively peaceful means, like economic sanctions or political pressure to open markets, to force or threats of force and even war. Such actions are always defended by expressions of dogma. Governments will claim that they have been compelled by circumstances not of their own making to attack or else be attacked. The citizenry is told that the dignity, sovereignty, and the safety of the nation are at stake. It is at these moments when political leaders are at the height of their popularity and influence. Appeals to blind the eyes of the many so that they can do for the few what the few would never dare do for themselves.

It is important to note that, often, the wealthy few are not themselves subject to dogma. Amassing wealth, which is their specialty, is a very rational business. They cannot thrive if they themselves are blinded by false realities and dogma. They would not themselves sacrifice their lives or interests in the name of patriotism. Rather the rational few use dogma to manipulate and exploit the common people. For the dominant groups, fundamental change such as global rule of law is extremely threatening. Their advantageous positions in society and their very way of life are dependent upon a changeless world of lawlessness. Through dogma they convince the rest of us that a world of inordinately wealthy people in every nation-state is natural, inevitable, and laudable. At these times they convince us that government is acting on behalf of all societal members and not just on behalf of the few. They continue to convince us that our freedoms and material wealth are due to the beloved changeless institutions that constitute much of our culture, and the role of power and greed are obscured. The nation-state reality serves all dominant groups the same way, whether the state is openly democratic or closed and totalitarian. The underlying benefits of lawlessness to the dominant group through nation-statehood are the same; only the power facades are different.

DEFICIENT ORGANISM

The stark reality is that our species may eventually come to a premature end. There is every reason to think that man and his earth will not exist forever. Also there is no reason to think that after this world there is another one that awaits us. There is reason to believe that our species still has a lot of living to do. However, in the time that will be allotted to us the many cannot just continue to exist for the benefit of the few. However long we have to live we all should live well. For each person to not live for himself or herself constitutes the greatest of obscenities. This finite existence of our species cannot just belong to the few through the trickery and deceit of religious and secular dogma. In figuring out how all of us can live better we will necessarily be figuring out how to avoid an unnecessary and uncalled for calamity. Our ability to live together as one species is not guaranteed. It must be earned through the increased application of reason. An over looked truth is that without law man is a deficient organism. If our somewhat developed minds have given us anything that might help save the day, it is the incite that attainment of the rule of law for all is imperative if a peaceful and constructive world is ever to be attained. In fact the rule of law worldwide is our only hope. There is no other way. The reality is that when there is no unifying law, man will act out his most immediate and least desirable tendencies. Without the rule of law differences between people, as well as political entities, are settled in a milieu of lawlessness and violence. Without law and order the social contract is obliterated and man lives in a jungle environment. Without enforceable law there is no trust among men and lawlessness is king. As with individuals, nations functioning without enforceable law become selfish, bullies and dangerous. Without law there really is no society, no cohesion. The present day nation-state system is neither a system nor a society of cohesive nations. Whether at the local level, state level, regional level, national level or international level, law and order is a requisite to civil life. There are no exceptions. There are no secondary options. For this reason political union among all of the peoples of earth must be viewed as our only serious option and not some pie in the sky dream. One species being subject to one government evokes fear in some people and chuckles in others. Those who feel fear do so because they have been programmed to think of a one government world as a dark totalitarian state that has the people of the world oppressed and enslaved. They envision a world without freedom and happiness. Those who chuckle over the notion of a one government world do so because they too have been programmed to believe that human beings have an evil nature that will simply not permit such a state. Further they cannot countenance a world of change and progress. They do not understand that their views of an evil nature in man and of a permanently stagnant static world are false ideas that have been programmed into them and created and sustained by relentless dogma. It may be a dream but it is an essential one. For on this realization rests the only hope of mankind for a better and brighter future. Political unification always involves compromises. To receive the benefits of a larger stronger union at times necessitates the loss of certain local prerogatives. If a federated system is properly designed the benefits will be magnified and the detriments minimized. Local control of local matters would by necessity and by right be left to local peoples. The global level of government would be concerned with global matters or matters effecting all citizens. Regional levels of government would handle regional matters. A one government world would not necessitate a situation where one central office would dictate the lives of local peoples. True individual freedom is the result of a composite of many factors. This global democratic government would insure individual freedom beyond anything heretofore experienced by man. At the moment political joinder even on a lesser stage always seems to be fraught with uncertainty and fear. How can we even begin to think about all of the billions of people inhabiting the entire planet actually living together in an orderly and peaceful manner under the rule of law? If it does not happen our species will continue to stagnate and atrophy. We actually have the ability to live together in an orderly and constructive way through the universal rule of law. This is predicated of course on man getting beyond dogma and the failed institutions it supports and maintains. Only until man can really think, only when man can think reasonably, only when dogma no longer clouds our minds with horrible nonsense will man ever be free to be himself. As secular and religious dogma erodes away, people will have less and less to fear in others. They will have less and less to mistrust in others. For their bond will be the human bond, a bond based on human thought and instinct. There will be no reason to advocate continued lawlessness. The advantages of order through law will be obvious to all. Only dogma and the fear and mistrust it produces stand in the way of human sanity and health. If world joinder is to be ultimately realized, it will be a slow, unchoreographed and almost imperceptible process. The path to a singular world government administering over those challenges of a global nature will indeed be a long one. The figurative path of which we speak will actually involve the slow and difficult process of nations individually at their own pace and within their own societies overcoming the many ways in which dogma has held them back. In this regard each nation will have its own successes and failures. As the institutional make up of each nation differs so will its challenges. The strategies and the vigor of each nation will reflect their own realities. Some nations will do better in some areas of change than others. Ultimately not all nations will arrive at the mature and healthy state that is required for greater world union at the same time. During this entire process each nation will of course continue to control its own destiny as an independent political entity. Each nation will proceed according to its own unique situation. This process will not resemble anything that has been orchestrated. Each nation's progress will be incremental and unsteady. Momentum will accelerate as individual societal members themselves move beyond dogma. An enlightened nation will not precede an enlightened populous. It will be a process where governments and other internal collectives catch up with individuals and this will enable even more individuals to move beyond the shadows of dogma. Much must be overcome. Dogma must be seen for what it is, a mere disguise for real thinking, reasoning and practical assessment making at every level. The status quo tricksters must be seen for what they are. The requisite vision enabling an escape from the detour of dogma and a return to the open highway of reason and instinct must be man's destiny. Without it he has none. With healthy instinct and real thinking man's view of tomorrow can be dramatically different than ever imagined.

THE WAY PAST LAWLESSNESS

Given the inherent lawlessness of the nation-state, we need to find a way past its deficiencies. It would be unrealistic to attempt to institute a world government overnight. Much change needs to occur before that day might arrive. A legitimate and authentic global government can never be imposed upon the people of the world. No outcome can be assured if force, violence, and power are the norm for deciding fundamental issues. A democratic government, irrespective of its size and its purview, must be the product of assent by its people, of shared acceptance of the values of individual liberty and of earned respect for the nature and structure of the government itself. These essential elements cannot be artificially forced upon the people by those trying to assert their will from the top.

In order to garner the free assent of people to global government, we must get past dogma. Dogma is at the foundation of each nation's stale institutions. In what way this process will occur depends upon both the nation and the institution in question. For example, religious belief may be overcome more quickly and more certainly in some nations than others. Inordinate wealth in the few will be harder to uproot in some societies than others. The foundation of a nation-state may be more dogmatically and historically rooted in some nations than others. Progress will be uneven, but it will be spurred on by individual human beings who have escaped Plato's cave and are ready to just be people, ready to just be a member of the human species, and ready to demand a fairer and brighter world for everyone. Only when reason and instinct have sufficiently replaced dogma and fear will the notion of a world government become relevant and be ripe for serious and concrete deliberations.

Development of a global government will probably be incremental. Unions less than a singular global government should be anticipated. These unions or partnerships will not themselves be full or complete political entities. Trust must be earned. The willingness and ability to work and live together must be cultivated over time. The nation-players themselves will have to be tested and continually recommitted. Adjustments will be made as partners see what works and what doesn't in the quest for a world based on greater order, fairness, and rationality.

Perhaps the most meaningful step toward world government will be our efforts, as citizens, to make our own countries more rational, pragmatic, and accountable for the needs and interests of all of its members. We should act to make government decision-making based on a rational and fair assessment of the needs of those most closely affected by policy as well as the short- and long-term interests of society as a whole. Being fair and reasonable is not a simple or easy task. But it will start with reforms that limit the undue influence and access of the few. As rational decision-making replaces dogma, the power of the inordinately wealthy over government will begin to wane, and as the power of the wealthy wanes, rational decision-making will become even stronger. Democracy will finally have the opportunity to function as intended, as a vehicle to free and protect everyone.

There will be a day, perhaps, when posterity will muse at the fuss that was required to attain the rule of law for all. At some point the notion of a singular government will be viewed by more and more peoples and nations as the only viable path for human society. At this very moment some billions of human beings around the earth are experiencing and enduring lives not fit for base animals. Others of billions of people work extremely hard and long and never earn enough money to provide for their families in health and dignity. Many others who are benefiting materially to one degree or another are still living unrewarding and depressing lives because of the engrained attitudes, biases, and tastes that are part and parcel of the rat race. Even the few at the top will someday awaken to the truth that they too could have lived more rewarding, meaningful, and natural lives. Direct and immediate consideration of implementing a world government will only take place toward the end of this desired historical process. For the time being continued incremental improvement of each society around the world is history's present task and our individual challenge.

SINGULAR GOVERNMENT

Given that a singular world government belongs to the distant future, it may seem premature to discuss what it actually might look like. But doing so is important. The dogmatists of today talk about world government as though it was a social-political armageddon. They think of it as a symbol of a world gone dark. It begins to stand for everything wrong with change. When people envision a one government world they do so through very programmed eyes. They are convinced that because of our permanent evil natures we as a species can never live peaceably and constructively together especially on the global stage. Some may even suggest it is because of the evil natures of those they do not know or understand that world peace and the life we love is unattainable on a global scope. Too often people conclude that plans for a one-government world must be a plot by the evildoers to deprive us of our way of life and all that we cherish about it, to strip us of all our important freedoms and make us slaves of the state. We would become objects of labor and have no real individual value.

These fears, however, stem from dogma, which clouds present thinking and biases people against any possible significant change in the future. Significant change is invariably seen as bad change. Present fear of the future becomes a present barrier to our thinking rationally about today as well as tomorrow. This suspicion of change must be countered with a more honest view of the possibilities and benefits of single government. What might a global government look like? First we must think of its size. Although the planet is vast and the population always growing, technology has brought us closer together. Travel technology alone has made us much closer. Pick out any two spots on the earth, and figure out how long it would have taken to get from one point to the other five hundred year ago. Next figure out how long it would take today to travel from one point to the other. Lastly, imagine how long it will take to go from one point to the other five hundred years from now. Communication technology has made similar leaps. The Internet has transformed world communication in just a short number of years. Think where this technology will be in five hundred years. A world polity would be much larger than anything else before it, but any problems presented by size and scope must be thought of as just challenges, challenges that we will be equipped to handle.

After size, we might think of the nature of its organization. The form and nature of world government must be such that it is capable of guaranteeing to all citizens of our world the value of the individual human being, the presence of personal choice, the necessity of a fair and meaningful opportunity to be what one can be, and sufficient wealth and health to make these benefits real and not just legal or political abstractions. But this does not imply a single government that regulates every part of human life. The US government is not the only government that the citizens of the United States possess. There are fifty state governments, hundreds of county and borough governments, and thousands of local or city governments. Each layer regulates the sphere that is appropriate to it. Likewise a global government would be charged with handling matters that affect all of the world. This might include everything from use of the world's natural resources, preventing war, and guaranteeing the freedom and well-being of individuals to dealing with global threats like asteroids or extraterrestrial life forms.

A third feature of global government must be democracy—specifically a democratic government that divides power. A first step would be the tripartite sharing of political power and responsibility in the three co-equal branches of the legislative, executive, and judicial. How these branches would be composed is a task for the future, but any organization must reflect the needs and interests of all types of people and have mechanism in place for oversight and reform. And it will be important to not simply utilize the nation-state divisions, which emerged in sometimes irrational and arbitrary ways. All government, at whatever level, would be representative government and their administrative, legislative, and judicial offices would be elected by the people of that particular jurisdiction. Each government would be answerable to the people of its jurisdiction. So as to never again permit the inordinately wealthy to own or control the affairs of government all elections at all levels would be paid for by taxpayers only. Private monies would not be allowable for any electoral or lobbying purposes. A global government must look like and function as a true democracy. This may involve far-reaching changes to our current model of democracy, like the elimination of political parties as we now know them or the replacement of representative democracy with direct democracy.

The key features will be the cooperation of people across the globe rather than the exploitation of the many by the few and the opportunity for all people to exercise individual freedom in its fullest and most mature sense. Dogma often tells us that the greatest threat to personal freedom is excessive government action and overreaching. But our freedom to develop our potential is threatened as much, if not more, by the stifling effects of inordinate wealth, dogma, and the lawlessness of the nation-state. The fundamental promise and directive of any world government must be the assurance of individual freedom and individual responsibility and the well-being of each human being on the planet.

Conclusion

It is difficult for most people to fully grasp the utter and complete interwoveness of the human organism and its surrounding world. This interconnectedness is not simply the one-sided "selflessness" espoused by much of Eastern thought. It is an acknowledgment of the true and unique individual who by its nature cannot be a singularity without at the same time being an integral part of the rest of the world. Although we are individuals, we can never separate ourselves from this earth or universe. We simply cannot blindly exist as a small cluster of particles detached from and unrelated to the unimaginable number of particles constituting the universe. The tension is not imagined. It is a product of our cerebral evolution. When recognition of this duality is achieved, then our being bound by and to this earth is less mysterious and less an earthly prison to be escaped from at death. We can perhaps each accept our individual life less as a burden and more as a gift that remains a challenge to be sure. It is only by viewing ourselves and the world we live in a dogmatic and distorted way that we justify our inability to devise and implement societal institutions that befit and are consonant with the essential natures and needs of all its member human beings. This distortion lies at the feet of dogma, both religious and secular.

To grasp the depth of the impact that religious make-believe, secular rationalization for tragic disparity in life opportunity, and continued contrived violence and turmoil have on the human being requires that we understand the human organism as it is. That begins with the knowledge that for a human being all that there is, is body. Mental activity is but an aspect of body and bodily forces. It is with this body and only with this body that each human being can know any reality and properly attempt to navigate through life. Through dogma body is fraudulently deprived of its rightful place as our own individual universe through which we share in the larger universe with all others.

Language and thought are inextricably woven together. They constitute a natural human tool and are as much a human tool as are eyes, ears, or noses. These natural bodily tools are meant to get us through life on earth. Language and thought, like other human tools, are not meant to be used for the construction of possible and imaginary worlds beyond. They are not adequate for discerning nonphysical or metaphysical worlds. As Wittgenstein wrote, "The sense of the world must lie outside the world. In the world everything is as it is, and everything happens as it does happen." The physical world is the only legitimate workplace for our faculties. They are not relevant beyond our actual physical world. Attempts to go beyond our world, through belief, is to engage in make-believe—a make-believe given birth and jealously maintained by incessant dogma.

Dogma takes root in us through early training. The ideas that children receive generally constitute who that person is throughout his or her life. This is because any serious new idea being weighed or considered as a replacement candidate is being judged by the very idea that may be replaced. Self-modification therefore becomes a precarious process indeed. Clearly the institutions of religion, wealth disparity, and the lawless nation-state all stand on dogmatic footings. These are the very dogmas implanted into each of us as children, which continue to reinforce their "rightness" throughout our lives, making us ever less able to question them. It becomes a vicious and obscene cycle.

Dogma often dominates the realm of religion. Dogma tries to obscure the fact that there is no actual and legitimate connection between a real god and religion. Instead it is clear religion is a human invention that has proven harmful to individuals and society as a whole. Morality is a requisite to societal formation and maintenance, but religion has appropriated morality as its own and holds itself out as its only source. The natural processes of the body that we frequently refer to as mind or spirit have likewise been appropriated by religious belief as eternal detachable soul. God itself has been victimized by religion. Religionists reduce the notion of god to the puny size of their own comprehension. By reconstituting humanity, the world, and god, religious distortion is complete. Without dogma, religious belief would be easily appreciated as what it is, a horrific relic of the past.

Another facet of dogma is the acceptance of inordinate wealth concentrated in the hands of the few. Rational thought shows that this concentration of wealth is unfair to individuals and also corrosive to authentic representative government. It undermines democracy and can make it all but a political illusion. Further, it is in conflict with a good working capitalistic model, a model that would be the basis for a fairer and more accessible capitalism. We must reject the economic dogmas that there is only so much to go around and that under any other system the average person would have it even worse. The favored position of the inordinately wealthy is maintained by one dogmatic doctrine after another. Only reason, real thinking, can rescue the many from the endless control and exploitation by the few. Without dogma, inordinate wealth in the few would be transformed into a benign and acceptable wealth disparity that no longer threatens democracy and representative government.

Finally, dogma has led us to accept the lawlessness of the nation-state. Because the nation-state is, by definition, not subject to any law save its own, it can never provide a basis for worldwide peace and cooperation. Even supranational organizations like the UN cannot overcome the lawlessness of the nation-state because it lacks any method of enforcement. Law and order is not possible unless there is a body that can legitimately enforce the law. This body is of course government. Global law and order requires a singular government. This government must necessarily be legitimate and truly democratic. For an enhancement of our well-being it is necessary that there be one law for one species and equal rights and opportunities for all. Without reason, or real thinking, in the affairs of human beings a more rational and healthy world may never be enjoyed and stagnation, atrophy, and perhaps a premature demise may well await our species.

In all of these realms—religion, economics, and governance—dogma is the enemy of rationality and progress. Dogma consists of the ideas and rhetoric that teach us to find laudable that which is not actually laudable, real that which is not real, and good that which is not good. Dogma contorts life itself in that our self-invented reality conforms to every requirement of accepted dogma. Dogma through carefully sculptured institutions tells us who we are, why we are here, and what we should do while we are here. However, by drawing on our natural instincts and reason, we can change our old and inadequate institutions so that they reflect the true interests of every single human being. It is revealing that this is still a brazen and radical idea.

Nature, reality, and truth deserve to be heard. This is a fight for our very nature and for what it can be to be human. The earth is where and what we are. It will not be here forever. It will end as will we. We therefore owe it to those who are yet to be to reinstitute instinct and reason, to get beyond incessant and relentless dogma and the institutions it has so carefully carved out for us. Our posterity deserves institutions that are actually consistent with the interests of everyone.

As human beings all that we possess naturally is for the purpose of navigating through life on this earth. As our various attributes enable us to develop, self-actualize, and endure for a time, they also function to limit us to nothing more, nothing bigger, and nothing better. We for the most part think and share ideas through language. The use of language may constitute real thinking if experience, logic, and reason are allowed to play their intended role. But language and thought become false masks when unsupported views, make-believe, and blind trust are given unwarranted legitimacy through dogma. By limiting what we can imagine, dogma imprisons us, limits our possibilities to those of the ugly past, and prevents any hope for a brighter tomorrow. Dogma has led us through the great and historical primrose path of ignorance, unimaginable wealth disparity, violence, and waste.

A world of real thought is a world of hope and optimism. New ideas bring new opportunities, new possibilities for what life could be like. What ails us cannot be fixed solely by science or technology. What ails us can only be completely fixed through the natural and general application and use of instinct and reason in all our affairs.

www.ingramcontent.com/pod-product-compliance
Lightning Source LLC
Chambersburg PA
CBHW050141240426
43673CB00043B/1750